Cookbook for the 90s

By Helen V. Fisher

FISHER
BOOKS

Publishers: Bill Fisher
                Helen Fisher
                Howard Fisher

Editors: Joyce Bush
                Bill Fisher

Book Production:
                Paula Peterson
                Nancy Taylor

Art Director: Josh Young
Drawings: David Fischer
Cover photo: DeGennaro Associates, Los Angeles

Published by Fisher Books
P.O. Box 38040
Tucson, AZ 85740-8040
602/744-6110

Copyright 1990 Fisher Books

Printed in U.S.A.
Printing 10 9 8 7 6

**Library of Congress
Cataloging-in-Publication Data**

Fisher, Helen V.
    Cookbook for the 90s / by Helen V. Fisher

        p.   cm.

    Includes index.

    ISBN 1-55561-038-2 (pbk.)

    1. Lowfat diet—Recipes. 2. Low-cholesterol
diet—Recipes. I. Title. II. Title: Cookbook for the
nineties.
RM237.7F57   1990
641.5'638—dc20   90-32226
                                        CIP

Table of Contents

Acknowledgments

I wish to thank Mable and Gar Hoffman for their generous help with recipe development. Over the past 15 years that I have worked with Mable and Gar, they have been sources of inspiration for me. I feel fortunate to have had their support in the preparation of this book. I also wish to thank Karen Ford Fisher for her help with recipe development and testing. I appreciate the time and effort she dedicated to this project.

An Introduction to
Cookbook for the 90s

Everywhere we turn we are being bombarded with new information about health, diet, exercise, foods and nutrition. Health-related newsletters abound, television and radio talk shows encourage us daily to change our ways. A bewildering amount of information is available and it's increasingly difficult to sift through this vast amount of material, picking out what's valid and what's just a fad.

In *Cookbook for the 90s*, I have tried to follow a reasonable course. It's a book that does not go to extremes or make rash promises. It is not a medical book, but a collection of good-tasting recipes and suggestions based upon sound published evidence.

I hope to encourage you to make modest and reasonable changes in food preparation and eating habits that should improve your health. My recipes are low in fat, sugar and sodium, and high in fiber and carbohydrates. I am a firm believer in seasoning with herbs rather than relying on salt. Even though I have used sugar and other sweeteners in recipes,

I like the natural flavor to come through without being overpowered by adding too much sweetness.

Food fads come and go very quickly, as do special diets. What we all need to do is examine our own diet and see where we can make lasting changes. Take an honest look at yourself and your eating habits, isn't there room for improvement?

During the last decade, we have become far more aware of the nutritional value of our foods. Historically we cared only for flavor, not really knowing or caring whether we were harming ourselves with overly rich foods. The newer laws requiring labeling of nutritional information give us the facts we previously couldn't get. We can now make a judgment if we want to purchase a particular item based upon its content.

Thanks to breakthroughs made by the medical and nutritional community, we now know fats in our diet greatly affect our health. In no uncertain terms, we are advised to limit our intake of saturated fats and cholesterol. These are mostly found in animal fats like butter or lard which are solid at room temperature. Also to be avoided or limited are egg yolks, whole-milk products with high fat content such as ice cream or cheeses, red meats, and chicken skin. Most vegetable oils are safe to use—the exception being coconut and palm oils. Reducing your intake of saturated fats is a very important dietary change.

Cholesterol has become an everyday topic of conversation. Organ meats, animal fats, egg yolks and some dairy products are all high in cholesterol. We're advised to limit our intake of these foods. It is important to know what your total cholesterol is and adjust your diet to get the number within an acceptable range.

Cooking oils and fats have received a great deal of attention. Seafood and vegetables supply us with the main groups of good unsaturated fats. Whichever oil you choose, use it sparingly. Use additional liquids like broth, wine or juices when braising or stewing dishes. I use vegetable cooking sprays to coat my baking pans as well as stove-top cookware.

Another term we've learned is omega-3 fatty acid, a substance that appears to help prevent heart disease. Researchers urge us to eat fish at least twice a week.

Preferred monounsaturated cooking oils and fats including;

    Avocado oil

    Canola (rapeseed) oil

    Cashews

    Olive oil

    Peanuts and peanut oil

    Peanut butter

Acceptable polyunsaturated cooking oils and fats including;

    Almonds

    Corn oil

    Cottonseed oil

    Fish

    Pecans

    Safflower oil

    Sesame oil

    Soybean oil

    Sunflower oil

    Walnut oil

The exceptionally beneficial omega-3 fatty acids are found in;

    Herring

    Mackerel

    Salmon

    Trout

    White tuna

Studies have been made comparing cuisines of cultures that traditionally use particular oils and fats. For example, the Mediterranean countries have relied upon olive oil and they have less heart disease than Northern Europeans who use large quantities of butter and lard. People who live close to the sea benefit from a diet rich in fish and seafood.

Oriental cuisines, also considered healthy, have always emphasized vegetables, fish, poultry and grains. Meats are used in small quantities; in many cases, it is a flavor enhancement for the other ingredients. When we continue our look at some of the healthier cultures and their cuisines, another difference becomes evident. They combine fruits and grains with meats and poultry. Whether intentional or not it does a good job of bringing more fiber into their diet.

Traditional "peasant" food is really very healthful. Simple dishes of corn, rice and beans, staples—to the poor throughout the world—is the basis of good eating.

Make an extra effort to enrich your meals with more fruits, cereals, legumes, poultry, vegetables and moderate amounts of nuts. Include fish at least two to three times per week. Limit your intake of lean well-trimmed red meats. You can learn to enjoy lowfat or nonfat milk products.

Food producers are keenly aware of changing appetites and are responding. Great breakthroughs are coming which will aid us in our search for combining " good tasting and good for us." A broad range of foods offering better flavor and fresh appearance are appearing in the refrigerated cases of our markets. Be sure to read the labels for ingredients as well as proper storage and expiration dates. Follow recommended cooking times.

With *Cookbook for the 90s* I hope to convince you—and your tastebuds—that delectable, tasty dishes don't need excessive amounts of fat, sugar and sodium. You can enjoy great flavorful food without guilt. All recipes have the nutritional breakdown to help you get started on a decade of delicious and healthy eating.

Let's make shopping easier for everyone. Here is a list of food items that you should always keep available in the cupboard, refrigerator or freezer. Having the necessary ingredients at hand simplifies trying new recipes.

Pantry List

Bagels, plain

Bran, oat, rice

Canned beans, vegetarian-style

Canned evaporated skimmed milk

Canola oil

Cheeses, lowfat, part skim milk

Chicken breasts, skinless

Chicken broth, lowfat, low-sodium

Chinese five spice

Club soda

Couscous

Crispbreads

Dried beans, black, navy, pinto, lentils

Dried fruits

Dry buttermilk

English muffins, regular or oat

Fish: cod, crab, halibut, herring, orange roughy, salmon, scallops, snapper, sole

Fresh fruits in season

Fruit juices: apple, orange, pineapple, tomato, etc.

Grains: barley oats, couscous, millet, oats, rice, whole wheat, quinoa

Herbs

Lowfat mayonnaise

Nonfat cottage cheese

Nonfat dry milk powder

Nonfat milk

Nonfat plain or fruit yogurt

Olive oil

Pasta, no-egg

Peanut butter

Popcorn

Puffed corn, rice, wheat cakes

Rabbit

Rice bran

Rice: brown, white, wild

Salsas

Shellfish: clams, crab, mussels, oysters, scallops

Soft diet margarine (with water listed as 1st ingredient)

Soy sauce, low-sodium

Spices: cinnamon, cloves, curry, ginger, lemon pepper, mustard, nutmeg, paprika

Tortillas, lard-free

Tuna, water-packed

Turkey breasts, skinless

Vegetable cooking spray

Vegetables of all types

Vinegars: apple cider, balsamic, fruit, herb, rice, wine

Documentation

Nutrient analysis was calculated using *The Food Processor II Nutrition & Diet Analysis System* software program, version 3.0, copyright 1988, 1990, by ESHA Research. It has a data base of 2400 foods and 30 nutrients and uses USDA and other scientific sources as the data source. Analysis does not include optional ingredients. Only the first choice ingredient is calculated. The higher number is used for the range in servings.

Abbreviations

Because words such as *carbohydrates* are too long to fit across the bottom of the recipe in chart form, we have abbreviated as follows:

Cal = Calories

Prot = Protein

Carb = Carbohydrates

Fib = Fiber

Tot. Fat = Total Fat

Sat. Fat = Saturated Fat

Chol = Cholesterol

Menus

Breakfast

Broiled grapefruit
Chocolate Pecan Waffles, 84
Syrup
Beverage

Orange juice
Oatmeal with raisins
Brown sugar
Beverage

Pineapple juice
Lowfat cottage cheese
Fresh peaches
Blackberries
Orange-Pecan Muffins, 87
Beverage

Grapefruit juice
Mango Bread, 92
Papaya with lemon
Beverage

Apple juice
Toasted plain bagel
Yogurt Cream Cheese, 3
Cherry preserves
Beverage

Cranapple juice
Cold cereal
Banana
Nonfat milk
Beverage

Pineapple-orange juice
Baked Apple Delight, 214
Mozzarella cheese
Toasted whole-grain bread
Beverage

Fresh fruit cup
Carrot-Raisin Loaf, 93
Yogurt Cream Cheese, 3
Joyce's Pineapple Cooler,
  240
Nonfat lemon yogurt
Raspberries or blackberries
Cold bran cereal
Beverage

Orange slices
Walnut-Sweet Potato
Pancakes, 83
Syrup
Beverage

Apricot nectar
Broiled trout
Sliced tomatoes
Cornmeal Rolls, 89
Beverage

Broiled pineapple slices
  with cinnamon
Scrambled egg substitute
  with fresh herbs
Tomato Salsa, 9
Flour tortillas
Beverage

Fresh melon slices
Strawberries
Nonfat strawberry yogurt
Date-Pistachio Bread, 91
Beverage

Cranberry juice
Raisin-Oat Bran Pancakes,
  81
Canadian bacon
Syrup
Beverage

Lunch

Tomato juice
Turkey Melba Salad, 56
French bread
Honey Dressing, 60
Beverage

Beef bouillon
Shrimp Broil, 157
Pineapple cottage-cheese
 salad
Apple slices
Beverage

Tuna Fish Sandwich, 235
Sliced tomatoes
Island Slaw, 47
Beverage

Couscous Fruit Salad, 44
Toasted pita bread
Crab Spread, 5
Beverage

Cream of Mushroom Soup,
 24
Rosy Broiled Chicken
Sandwich, 233
Fresh fruit
Beverage

Classic Gazpacho, 26
Crab and Pasta, 47
French bread
Beverage

Lentil Soup, 21
Dark rye bread
Mixed green salad
Fresh pear
Beverage

Home-Style Vegetable Soup,
 19
Crispbread
Winter Salad, 53
Marmalade Dressing, 61
Beverage

Pumpkin Spice Soup, 28
Fennel Spinach Salad, 45
Italian Dressing, 63
Mediterranean Toast, 6
Beverage

Beef and Bean Burgers, 230
Lettuce
Tomatoes
Whole-wheat buns
Orange wedges
Beverage

Favorite Turkey Chili, 196
Lettuce
Cucumber slices
Toasted English muffin
Mixed fruit cup
Beverage

Monterey Chicken Salad, 185
Flour tortillas
Avocado Cream, 2
Pineapple slices
Beverage

Scallop Kabobs, 155
Cherry tomatoes
Spicy Green Beans, 130
Grapes
Beverage

Barbecue Bean Salad, 38
Crispbread
Banana slices
Beverage

Artichoke Chowder, 16
Greek Salad, 46
Crusty bread
Marshmallow Cupcakes, 209
Beverage

Dinner

Orange Roughy, 151
Twice-Baked Potatoes, 135
Beets with Raisins, 124
Mixed green salad
House Salad Dressing, 62
Blackberry-Lemon Bars,
    202
Beverage

Rosemary-Orange Chicken,
    132
Old-Fashioned Potato Salad,
    42
Corn on the cob
French bread
Angel food cake
Fresh fruit
Beverage

Albondigas, 17
Turkey Burros, 195
Three-Pepper Salad, 50
Mexican Rice, 102
Tortillas
Apricot Pudding, 213
Beverage

Stuffed Pork Tenderloin, 127
Brussels Sprouts,125
Steamed carrots
Mixed green salad
Favorite French Dressing, 59
Baked Apple Delight, 214
Beverage

Boston Beans, 105
Blue Corn Muffins, 85
Island Slaw, 47
Peaches & Cream Frozen
    Yogurt, 223
Fruit Bon Bons, 229
Beverage

Fillets Pacifica, 148
Pineapple Salsa, 74
Steamed rice
Asparagus
Sliced tomatoes
Blueberry Plum Pudding,
    211
Beverage

Chicken Cilantro, 179
Sunshine Salad, 49
Steamed carrots
Sliced tomatoes
Lemon-Poppy Seed Biscuits,
    90
Papaya Raspberry Pie, 206
Beverage

Oriental Vegetable Soup, 23
Yakitori Chicken, 193
Steamed rice
Steamed snow peas
Fruit Salad Dessert, 215
Beverage

Seafood Casserole, 158
Asparagus
Summer Fruit Salad, 52
Toasted bagels
Chocolate Mold, 222
Beverage

Steak in Plum Sauce, 170
Cooked rice noodles
Zucchini Salad, 51
Green peas
Sliced tomatoes
Stuffed Plums, 217
Beverage

Caribbean Cod, 145
Pilaf, 103
Baked Vegetable Medley,
    138
Crusty French bread
Lemon-Date Tart, 207
Beverage

Rabbit Provencal, 173
Pasta
Steamed Brussels sprouts
Red Cabbage à la Orange,
    127
Italian bread
Pears with Chocolate Sauce,
    216
Beverage

Corned Leg of Lamb, 164
Green Bean-Potato Salad, 40
Winter Salad, 53
French Bread
Chocolate Snowballs, 203
Beverage

Iced Parsley Soup, 27
Red Snapper, 152
Broccoli or green beans
Golden Rice, 101
Mixed green salad
Lemon Gingerbread, 210
Beverage

Appetizers

An appetizer is meant to stimulate your appetite. It can be either a food or drink served before the meal. Allow extra time to enjoy this pleasant way of introducing the meal to come.

Serve the appetizer in a room other than the dining room to set it apart from the dinner. During warm weather appetizers can be served on a porch or patio. This is a relaxed way to introduce guests to one another. Winter's chill causes you to think of a warm, friendly place indoors to begin your entertaining. Consider the living room or den, which is especially nice if it has a fireplace. If your guests enjoy helping, you can begin in the kitchen and invite their participation in preparing or serving. Be guided by the type of guests as well as the occasion.

Fresh vegetables are always appreciated by health-conscious guests. Cut them in attractive shapes and present them with Crab Spread. I like to accompany them with Mediterrean Toast.

Offer a choice of items that will complement the meal. Don't expect a single appetizer will please everyone. If possible, find out some of your guests' favorite foods beforehand and let that be your guide.

Follow a theme and you'll be surprised how easily it works. As a prelude to a Mexican Fiesta, begin with Jícama Canadian Bacon Spread or Avocado Cream and toasted flour-tortilla wedges.

Always present your appetizers in an attractive way. This need not be fancy, but it should be inviting.

Avocado Cream

Capers and pistachios add a surprising flavor to this delicate avocado spread.

1/2 medium avocado, peeled

1/2 cup Yogurt Cream Cheese, page 3

1 teaspoon lemon zest

2 teaspoons lemon juice

2 tablespoons pistachios

2 teaspoons cilantro (Chinese parsley)

2 teaspoons capers

Mash avocado and cream cheese together until blended; stir in remaining ingredients. Serve on toasted pita bread or bagels. Makes 1 cup.

Each tablespoon contains:

Cal	Prot	Carb	Fib	Tot. Fat	Sat. Fat	Chol	Sodium
18	1g	1g	1g	1g	0	0	3mg

Yogurt Cream Cheese

A substitute for cream cheese in recipes or use as a spread.

2 cups nonfat plain yogurt

Suggested Additions:

Chopped fresh or dried herbs

Chopped fresh or dried fruit

Honey

Fruit or maple syrup

Toasted Nuts

For snacks or a spread for crackers, add chopped fruit, fresh or dried. Season to taste with herbs or spices. Stir in honey, or fruit or maple syrup with your favorite toasted nuts.

Caution: Do not use yogurt that contains gelatin because it will not separate and drain properly.

Line a sieve or colander with 3 layers of cheesecloth or a paper coffee filter. Place sieve in a bowl to drain. Add yogurt. Cover; let drain in refrigerator 4 to 8 hours. Discard liquid. Use as cream cheese. Makes 1 cup.

Each tablespoon contains:

Cal	Prot	Carb	Fib	Tot. Fat	Sat. Fat	Chol	Sodium
16	2g	2g	0	0	0	1mg	22mg

Jícama Canadian Bacon Spread

For that final touch at serving time, sprinkle top of spread with finely chopped green onion.

4 oz. Canadian bacon

1 tablespoon white wine vinegar

1 teaspoon chicken bouillon granules

3 (4- to 5-inch) lengths trimmed green onions (include both green and white portions)

1 cup nonfat or lowfat cottage cheese

1/4 teaspoon celery seed

1/8 teaspoon pepper

4 to 5 oz. jícama, peeled and coarsely chopped

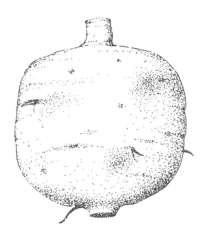

Bake Canadian bacon covered in 350F (175C) oven about 30 minutes. Cool; chop and set aside. In a small custard or measuring cup combine vinegar and chicken granules. Stir until granules are almost dissolved; set aside. In a blender or food processor fitted with a metal blade, combine onion, cottage cheese, celery seed, pepper and vinegar-bouillon mixture. Purée until smooth. Pour purée into 1-quart bowl; stir in bacon and jícama. Cover and refrigerate until serving time. Serve with crackers or party rye bread. Makes about 2 cups.

Each tablespoon contains:

Cal	Prot	Carb	Fib	Tot. Fat	Sat. Fat	Chol	Sodium
12	2g	1g	0	0	0	2mg	117mg

Crab Spread

Good on vegetables, crackers or toasted bagels

1/4 cup Yogurt Cream Cheese, page 3

2 tablespoons nonfat plain yogurt

2 tablespoons nonfat cottage cheese

2 teaspoons lemon juice

2 tablespoons chopped pimiento

3 tablespoons capers

1 teaspoon horseradish

1 green onion, chopped

3 oz. cooked crab

Dill weed to taste

In a small bowl blend Yogurt Cream Cheese with yogurt, cottage cheese and lemon juice. Stir in remaining ingredients. Cover and refrigerate until ready to serve. Serve with toasted pita wedges or crackers. Makes about 1 cup.

Each tablespoon contains:

Cal	Prot	Carb	Fib	Tot. Fat	Sat. Fat	Chol	Sodium
9	2g	0	0	0	0	5mg	27mg

Mediterranean Toast

Once you've tasted this, you'll prefer it to buttered toast.

6 French bread slices

1/4 cup olive oil

1/2 teaspoon garlic powder

1 tablespoon chopped fresh parsley

1/2 teaspoon dried-leaf oregano

1 teaspoon toasted sesame seeds

1/4 teaspoon paprika

Place bread slices on baking sheet. Preheat broiler or toaster oven. In a small bowl thoroughly combine remaining ingredients until well blended. Brush each slice of bread with mixture. Place under broiler and brown, turn slices and brush again. Return to broiler. Toast until brown. Serve at once. Makes 6 servings.

Each serving contains:

Cal	Prot	Carb	Fib	Tot. Fat	Sat. Fat	Chol	Sodium
184	4g	18g	1g	11g	2g	0	204mg

Vegetable Dip

Serve with toasted pita bread wedges.

1/2 cup lowfat cottage cheese

1/2 cup Yogurt Cream Cheese, page 3

3 sun-dried tomatoes, chopped

2 tablespoons lemon juice or vinegar

2 green onions, chopped

1/4 cup chopped green chiles

1/2 teaspoon dry mustard

2 teaspoons capers

1 teaspoon caper juice

1/4 cup chopped red bell pepper

In a bowl combine all ingredients. Pour into 2-cup serving container; cover and refrigerate several hours before serving. Makes 1-1/4 cups.

Each tablespoon contains:

Cal	Prot	Carb	Fib	Tot. Fat	Sat. Fat	Chol	Sodium
20	1g	2g	0	1g	0	0	27mg

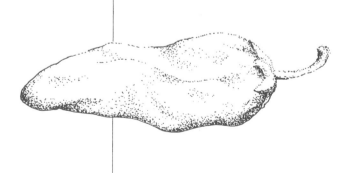

Tuna Dip

Another good way to use small amounts of leftovers. Enjoy this with crispbread and fresh vegetable sticks.

2 tablespoons water-pack tuna, drained

1/2 cup plain nonfat yogurt

1 teaspoon reduced-calorie mayonnaise

1 green onion, chopped

1/4 teaspoon garlic powder

1/4 teaspoon dill weed

1 teaspoon chopped parsley

2 teaspoons pimento

2 teaspoons prepared pickle relish

In a small bowl combine tuna, yogurt and mayonnaise, breaking tuna into small pieces. Stir in remaining ingredients. Cover and refrigerate until ready to use. Makes 3/4 cup.

Each tablespoon contains:

Cal	Prot	Carb	Fib	Tot. Fat	Sat. Fat	Chol	Sodium
11	1g	1g	0	0	0	2mg	24mg

Avocado Shrimp Mousse

Present this in an attractive mold.

2 (1/4-oz.) pkgs. unflavored gelatin

3/4 cup chicken broth

3/4 cup skimmed evaporated milk

3 tablespoons lemon juice

1 tablespoon cider vinegar

1 ripe avocado

2 green onions, chopped

1 tablespoon chopped pimiento

1 (6-oz.) can cocktail shrimp

1/4 teaspoon Tabasco sauce or to taste

Salt and lemon pepper to taste

Tomato Salsa, page 75

In a small saucepan sprinkle gelatin over chicken broth. Heat, stirring until gelatin dissolves. Pour broth, milk, lemon juice and vinegar into a food processor or blender. Peel avocado, remove seed and add to mixture with green onion. Process until smooth. Stir in pimiento, shrimp, Tabasco sauce, salt and lemon pepper to taste. Spray a 3-cup mold with vegetable cooking spray. Pour mixture into mold. Cover and refrigerate until set. Serve with Tomato Salsa. Makes 6 (1-/2 cup) servings.

Each serving contains:

Cal	Prot	Carb	Fib	Tot. Fat	Sat. Fat	Chol	Sodium
129	12	7g	4g	6g	1g	50mg	90mg

Mediterranean Vegetable Appetizer

Use sun-dried tomatoes without oil for a low-calorie appetizer.

2 tablespoons canola or olive oil

1 onion, chopped

1/2 cup sun-dried tomatoes, cut into thin strips

1 carrot, shredded

1 green or yellow pepper, seeded and finely chopped

1 eggplant, minced, peeled

1 teaspoon salt

1/4 teaspoon pepper

1 teaspoon sugar

1 teaspoon red wine vinegar

2 tablespoons chopped fresh cilantro (Chinese parsley)

Pita bread rounds

In a large skillet heat oil. Add onions; sauté 2 or 3 minutes. Stir in tomatoes, carrot, green or yellow pepper, eggplant, salt, pepper, sugar and vinegar. Simmer 15 to 20 minutes, stirring occasionally, until vegetables are tender. Stir in cilantro. Cut each pita round into 6 or 8 wedges. Let each person spoon vegetable mixture on pita wedges. Makes about 3 cups.

Each tablespoon contains:

Cal	Prot	Carb	Fib	Tot. Fat	Sat. Fat	Chol	Sodium
9	0	1g	0	1g	0	0	45mg

Broccoli Flowers

*Make ahead to serve as "pick-up"
food at a buffet or picnic.*

1 lb. fresh broccoli

**1 (5-oz.) pkg. very thinly sliced
cooked chicken (about 20 slices)**

**2 tablespoons grated Romano
cheese**

**1 tablespoon reduced-calorie
mayonnaise**

1 tablespoon plain nonfat yogurt

1/2 teaspoon Dijon-style mustard

Trim broccoli; cut flowers and stems
into about 20 (3- to 4-inch long)
pieces. Cook in boiling water about
5 minutes or until tender; drain.
While hot sprinkle with cheese.
Spread one side of chicken slices
with a combination of mayonnaise,
yogurt and mustard. Place one
length of cooked broccoli in center
of each chicken slice. Roll up like a
cornucopia with broccoli flower pro-
truding through the open end. Serve
warm or cold. Makes 6 servings.

Each serving contains:

Cal	Prot	Carb	Fib	Tot. Fat	Sat. Fat	Chol	Sodium
73	8g	5g	2g	3g	1g	14mg	201mg

Fruity Barbecue Turkey Pick-ups

A surprise flavor combination that will result in requests for the recipe.

1/2 cup thick hickory smoke barbecue sauce

1 (8-oz.) can jellied cranberry sauce

1 (8-oz.) can crushed pineapple, drained

1/2 teaspoon grated fresh ginger root

1 teaspoon honey

3 cups cubed, skinned, cooked turkey

In a medium saucepan combine barbecue sauce, cranberry sauce, pineapple, ginger root and honey. Stir over low heat until cranberry sauce dissolves. Add turkey and continue cooking until hot. Have wooden picks handy for serving. Makes about 45 turkey pieces.

Each piece with white meat contains:

Cal	Prot	Carb	Fib	Tot. Fat	Sat. Fat	Chol	Sodium
28	3g	3g	0	0	0	6mg	30mg

Each piece with dark meat contains:

Cal	Prot	Carb	Fib	Tot. Fat	Sat. Fat	Chol	Sodium
30	3g	3g	0	1g	0	8mg	32mg

Italian Treasure Meatballs

Let your guests discover what is tucked inside.

1/2 lb. select ground beef

1 green onion, chopped

1/4 cup rice bran

1 egg white

2 teaspoons capers

1/2 teaspoon dried-leaf basil

1/2 teaspoon dried-leaf marjoram

1 tablespoon chopped parsley

1 tablespoon tomato sauce

Salt and pepper to taste

20 pimiento-stuffed olives

Preheat oven to 375F (190C). In a small bowl combine beef, green onion, rice bran, egg white, capers, basil, marjoram, parsley and tomato sauce. Thoroughly mix ingredients. Take a scant tablespoon full of meat mixture and pat into a patty; press one olive in center. Pinch meat around olive. Place on ungreased cookie sheet. Repeat with remaining olives. Bake 25 to 30 minutes. Makes 20 meatballs.

Each meatball contains:

Cal	Prot	Carb	Fib	Tot. Fat	Sat. Fat	Chol	Sodium
40	3g	1g	0	3g	1g	10mg	110mg

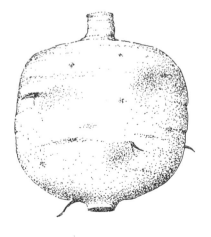

Soups

Homemade soup brings back memories of home and tasty, nourishing simple meals. Homemade soup is what I grew up with; it wasn't until I was a teenager that I tasted canned soups. They didn't compare to my mother's soups. For something out of the ordinary, serve Chestnut Soup or Artichoke Chowder.

Cold soups are probably enjoyed most during warm weather. We seem to always be looking for the winning combination of something easy to fix, prepare ahead and be well received by all. These are often referred to as *a salad you can spoon.*

I like to serve cold soups like Cantaloupe, Iced Parsley or Gazpacho on the patio. To keep it chilled on a warm day, place the serving bowl within a larger bowl filled with ice. Have a tray with garnishes, cups and a ladle for stirring and serving. Let each person garnish his own.

Cream soups can help turn a small portion of leftovers, usually vegetables, into a satisfying dish. Served in a cup for a starter or in a bowl for lunch, soup is always welcome. In some Middle European and Far Eastern countries, soup is served for breakfast, a pleasant and nutritious way to start the day.

Albondigas, a Mexican soup, is an example of a complete meal in a bowl. If this is new to you, be adventuresome and try it.

Basic stock recipes are included for preparing your own Beef, Chicken and Vegetarian Broths. Make them when time is available and freeze them in small containers for future use. Adjust the vegetables and seasoning to your family's preferences. I want these recipes to serve as a starting point that you can build on.

Artichoke Chowder

A different combination of subtle flavors.

1 tablespoon olive oil

1/2 cup chopped onions

1 cup sliced mushrooms

1 (8-oz.) can artichokes, chopped, drained

2 cups chicken broth

1/2 cup green peas

4 tablespoons all-purpose flour

2 cups evaporated skimmed milk

Salt and pepper to taste

In a large saucepan heat oil, sauté onions. Add mushrooms, artichokes and broth. Cook about 5 minutes until tender. Add peas. Blend flour in evaporated milk; add to mixture and cook 5 to 7 minutes until slightly thickened. Season to taste with salt and pepper. Makes 5 (1-cup) servings.

Each serving contains:

Cal	Prot	Carb	Fib	Tot. Fat	Sat. Fat	Chol	Sodium
186	13g	26g	5g	4g	1g	4mg	162mg

Albóndigas

A traditional Mexican soup made with turkey rather than beef.

1/2 lb. skinless turkey, ground

1/4 onion, chopped

1 egg white

1/4 cup quick-cooking rice

8 cups chicken broth

4 cups water

1/4 cup tomato sauce

2 whole roasted chiles, chopped

1 fresh tomato, chopped

1 carrot, julienned

2 green onions, cut in 2-inch lengths

1/4 teaspoon dried-leaf oregano

1/3 cup frozen corn kernels

2 tablespoons fresh chopped cilantro (Chinese parsley)

In a small bowl combine turkey, chopped onion, egg white and rice. Take about 1 tablespoon of mixture and form into 1-inch balls. Set aside. In a 4-quart pot combine broth, water, tomato sauce, chilies, tomato, carrot, green onions, oregano and corn. Bring mixture to a boil. Add meatballs, reduce heat and simmer about 30 minutes. Add cilantro and cook 5 minutes more. Serve hot. Makes 10 (1-cup) servings.

Each serving contains:

Cal	Prot	Carb	Fib	Tot. Fat	Sat. Fat	Chol	Sodium
108	11g	6g	1g	4g	1g	16mg	67mg

Dilled Vegetable Soup

This soup is especially good with warm corn bread or Blue Corn Muffins, page 85.

4 cups Vegetable Stock, page 36

1 teaspoon dill weed

Dash of pepper

1-1/2 cups diced potatoes

1/2 cup diced onion

3 carrots, sliced 1/4-inch thick

2 cups sliced zucchini

2 tomatoes, chopped

Salt to taste

Combine stock, dill weed, pepper, potatoes, onion and carrots in a 2-quart saucepan. Bring mixture to full boil, partially cover, reduce heat and simmer 20 minutes. Add zucchini and tomatoes and cook 10 minutes longer or until all vegetables are tender. Salt to taste. Serve hot. Makes 6 (1-cup) servings.

Each serving contains:

Cal	Prot	Carb	Fib	Tot. Fat	Sat. Fat	Chol	Sodium
107	3g	22g	4g	2g	0	0	19mg

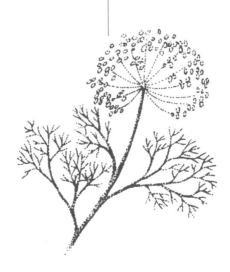

Home-Style Vegetable Soup

Warm and satisfying, a meal that is ideal for a cold day.

1 tablespoon olive oil

1 onion, chopped

2 celery stalks, chopped

2 carrots, sliced

1 zucchini, sliced

1/2 cup canned garbanzo beans (chick peas)

1 (8-oz.) can tomatoes with juice

2 bay leaves

1/2 teaspoon Italian herbs

2 cups chicken broth

1 cup tomato juice

5 cups water

1 tablespoon fresh chopped parsley

1/2 cup fresh sliced mushrooms

2 cups fresh chopped spinach

1 cup cooked pasta

In a 4-quart pot heat oil. Sauté onion, celery and carrots. Add zucchini, garbanzo beans, tomatoes with juice, bay leaves, Italian herbs, broth, tomato juice and water. Bring to a boil, reduce heat and cook over medium heat until vegetable are tender, about 30 minutes. Add parsley, mushrooms, spinach and pasta. Cook another 7 to 10 minutes. Remove and discard bay leaves. Makes 8 (1-cup) servings.

Each serving contains:

Cal	Prot	Carb	Fib	Tot. Fat	Sat. Fat	Chol	Sodium
100	5g	16g	3g	3g	0	0	184mg

Chestnut Soup

Chestnuts can be purchased fresh, canned or vacuum packed.

2 teaspoons canola oil

1/2 onion, chopped

1 carrot, sliced

1 celery stalk, sliced

4 cups chicken broth

1 teaspoon sugar

1 bay leaf

1/4 teaspoon dried-leaf basil

1/8 teaspoon dried-leaf marjoram

24 (1/2 lb.) chestnuts, shelled, roasted

1/2 cup evaporated skimmed milk

3/4 cup marsala, sherry or chicken broth

Salt and pepper to taste

In a large pot heat oil and sauté onion, carrot and celery. Add broth, sugar, bay leaf, basil, marjoram and chestnuts. Simmer until chestnuts are tender, about 25 minutes. Remove and discard bay leaf. Carefully transfer to a food processor or blender and purée mixture. Return to pot and stir in evaporated milk, bring to a boil; add marsala, sherry or chicken broth. Season to taste with salt and pepper. Serve hot or cold. Makes 6 (1-cup) servings.

Each serving contains:

Cal	Prot	Carb	Fib	Tot. Fat	Sat. Fat	Chol	Sodium
205	6g	29g	6g	3g	1g	2mg	38mg

Lentil Soup

Extra spice adds zest to this hearty dish.

1 cup dried lentils

1/2 onion, chopped

1/2 teaspoon cardamom

1 carrot, sliced

1 celery stalk, sliced

1/2 teaspoon pepper

1 red bell pepper, sliced

1/2 teaspoon cinnamon

4 cups Vegetable Stock, page 36, or water

1 (16-oz.) can tomatoes

1 (10-oz.) pkg. frozen broccoli spears

Salt to taste

Rinse and sort lentils. In a saucepan or Dutch oven combine lentils, onions, cardamom, carrots, celery, pepper, bell peppers, cinnamon and stock. Bring to a boil. Cover, reduce heat and simmer about 30 minutes or until lentils are done. Add tomatoes and broccoli, cook until tender. Salt to taste. Serve hot. Makes 8 (1-cup) servings.

Each serving contains:

Cal	Prot	Carb	Fib	Tot. Fat	Sat. Fat	Chol	Sodium
149	10g	27g	6g	2g	0	0	111mg

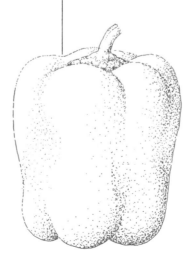

Moussaka Soup

*Rich flavor marks this
wholesome soup.*

1 small eggplant

4 tablespoons olive oil

8 cups Lamb Stock, page 35

1/2 lb. cooked lamb, cubed

1/4 teaspoon salt

1/2 teaspoon dried-leaf oregano

2 large tomatoes, chopped

1/2 cup frozen peas

**Grated Parmesan cheese for
garnish**

Peel eggplant and cut into 1/2-inch
cubes. Heat olive oil in a 2-1/2-quart
saucepan and brown eggplant. Add
stock, lamb, salt and oregano. Bring
to a full boil. Reduce heat, cover and
simmer 5 minutes or until eggplant
is very soft. Add tomatoes and peas
and cook 2 minutes longer. Serve
hot with garnish of grated Parmesan
cheese. Makes 5 (1-cup) servings.

Each serving contains:

Cal	Prot	Carb	Fib	Tot. Fat	Sat. Fat	Chol	Sodium
295	22g	9g	3g	19g	5g	41mg	166mg

Oriental Vegetable Soup

Chicken and pork make a flavorful combination.

1 tablespoon canola oil

1 tablespoon ginger root

1 chicken thigh, skinned

1/2 lb. cubed, fat-trimmed lean pork tenderloin

6 cups Chicken Stock, page 34

3 green onions, chopped

1 (10-oz.) pkg. frozen leaf spinach, thawed

1 (8-1/2-oz.) can water chestnuts, sliced, drained

1/4 lb. fresh mushrooms, sliced

1/4 lb. fresh or 2 cups canned bean sprouts, rinsed, drained

2 teaspoons low-sodium soy sauce

Salt and pepper to taste

Heat oil and ginger root in a 5- to 6-quart pot. Add chicken and pork, lightly brown. Add stock and green onions, bring to a full boil. Reduce heat and simmer 20 minutes. Add spinach and simmer 3 minutes. Add water chestnuts and mushrooms. Continue cooking 5 minutes or until mushrooms are tender. Add bean sprouts, cover and cook 2 to 3 minutes. Stir in soy sauce. Season to taste with salt and pepper. Serve at once. Makes 12 (1-cup) servings.

Each serving contains:

Cal	Prot	Carb	Fib	Tot. Fat	Sat. Fat	Chol	Sodium
122	13g	5g	2g	6g	2g	29mg	102mg

Cream of Mushroom Soup

Combine different types of mushrooms for an interesting appearance.

1 lb. fresh mushrooms

3 tablespoons margarine

4 cups Vegetable Stock, page 36

1/2 teaspoon dried-leaf basil

2 cups evaporated skimmed milk

1/2 cup flour

1/4 cup white wine

Salt and pepper to taste

Rub mushrooms with a damp paper towel. Trim mushrooms, slice or chop them in small pieces. In a 3- to 4-quart saucepan melt margarine, add mushrooms. Stirring frequently cook mushrooms until lightly brown. Add vegetable stock and basil. Heat to boiling, simmer gently 30 minutes. Remove pan from heat. Blend evaporated milk and flour together; add to mixture. Return pan to heat; stir and simmer until soup thickens. Add wine. Do not allow soup to boil again. Season to taste with salt and pepper. Serve hot. Makes 6 (1-cup) servings.

Each serving contains:

Cal	Prot	Carb	Fib	Tot. Fat	Sat. Fat	Chol	Sodium
215	11g	29g	3g	6g	1g	3mg	172mg

Cantaloupe Cooler

This soup tends to separate, so stir well before serving.

1 medium cantaloupe (2 lb.)

1-1/2 cups orange juice

1/4 teaspoon salt

1/4 teaspoon ground ginger

1 tablespoon lime juice

1 (5-1/3-oz.) can sweetened condensed milk

Fresh mint sprigs for garnish

1 lime, thinly sliced, for garnish

Cut cantaloupe in half. Remove peel and seeds; slice in wedges and chop. Put cantaloupe and remaining ingredients in blender or food processor, purée until smooth. Refrigerate several hours. Stir before serving. Serve cold with garnish of fresh mint or lime slices. Makes 8 (1/2-cup) servings.

Each serving contains:

Cal	Prot	Carb	Fib	Tot. Fat	Sat. Fat	Chol	Sodium
122	3g	25g	1g	2g	1g	6mg	101mg

Classic Gazpacho

Ideal for warm weather. This soup can be kept for 5 days in your refrigerator.

2-1/2 cups beef broth

4 cups vegetable-juice cocktail

1 cup chopped onion

1-1/2 cups chopped green pepper

1 garlic clove, minced

1/8 teaspoon Tabasco sauce

1 tablespoon Worcestershire sauce

1 cup diced tomato

1 celery stalk, diced

Chopped green pepper for garnish

Chopped green onions for garnish

Diced tomato

Diced celery

Diced cucumber

Chopped ripe avocado

Croutons for garnish

Combine broth and vegetable-juice cocktail in a 3-quart bowl. In a blender purée 1 cup broth/vegetable-juice-cocktail mixture with onion, 3/4 cup green pepper, garlic, Tabasco sauce and Worcestershire sauce. Add puréed mixture to bowl, stir well. Stir in remaining green pepper, tomato and celery. Refrigerate several hours. Serve cold with garnish tray containing more green pepper, onion, tomato, celery and cucumber as well as chopped ripe avocado and croutons. Makes 8 (1-cup) servings.

Each serving contains:

Cal	Prot	Carb	Fib	Tot. Fat	Sat. Fat	Chol	Sodium
48	2g	10g	2g	0	0	0	578mg

Iced Parsley Soup

*Your family or guests will welcome a
pretty, cool soup to begin a meal.*

3 tablespoons margarine

**1 medium onion, peeled and
chopped**

3 cups Chicken Stock, page 34

1/8 teaspoon ground pepper

1 cup plain nonfat yogurt

1 cup chopped fresh parsley

**4 teaspoons toasted slivered
almonds**

Heat margarine in a 2-quart saucepan. Add chicken stock and sauté
onion. Heat to simmering, cook
5 minutes. Cool slightly. Pour onion-
stock mixture into blender or food
processor. Add yogurt and purée.
Stir in parsley. Refrigerate several
hours. Serve cold. Garnish with
almonds. Makes 8 (1/2-cup)
servings.

Each serving contains:

Cal	Prot	Carb	Fib	Tot. Fat	Sat. Fat	Chol	Sodium
76	4g	5g	1g	5g	1g	1mg	78mg

Pumpkin Spice Soup

Prepare this in the morning and enjoy it for lunch or dinner.

1 (16-oz.) can pumpkin

2 (13-oz.) cans evaporated skimmed milk

1 tablespoon molasses

1/2 cup light corn syrup

1/2 teaspoon salt

1/2 teaspoon pumpkin-pie spice

Nutmeg for garnish

Place all ingredients in a 2-1/2- to 3-quart mixer bowl. Beat until well blended. Refrigerate several hours. Stir before serving. Sprinkle with nutmeg for garnish. Makes 8 (3/4-cup) servings.

Each serving contains:

Cal	Prot	Carb	Fib	Tot. Fat	Sat. Fat	Chol	Sodium
154	7g	32g	1g	0	0	4mg	252mg

Sweet and Spicy Carrot Soup

If you prefer a sweeter taste, add 2 teaspoons sugar before chilling.

1-1/2 cups cold water

1/2 teaspoon salt

1 (16-oz.) pkg. frozen carrots

1-1/2 cups orange juice

1/2 teaspoon nutmeg

1 cup chicken broth

1 orange, thinly sliced for garnish

Mint sprigs for garnish

Combine water, salt and carrots in a 2-1/2-quart saucepan; cover and bring to a boil. Reduce heat, simmer carrots 8 to 10 minutes or until carrots are very soft. Remove from heat and let cool. In a blender or food processor purée carrots and cooking liquid. In a large bowl combine puréed carrots with orange juice, nutmeg and broth; mix well. Cover bowl and refrigerate 2 hours or until well chilled. Serve cold with garnish of fresh orange slice and mint sprig. Makes 8 servings.

Each serving contains:

Cal	Prot	Carb	Fib	Tot. Fat	Sat. Fat	Chol	Sodium
47	2g	10g	2g	0	0	0	167mg

Zucchini Cooler

Here's another way to prepare versatile zucchini.

3 medium zucchini

2 cups beef broth or Beef Stock, page 33

1/2 teaspoon dill weed

1/8 teaspoon garlic powder

1 cup plain nonfat yogurt

1 cup evaporated skimmed milk

Raw zucchini slices for garnish

Chopped pimiento for garnish

Parsley for garnish

Salt and pepper to taste

Wash zucchini and cut in 1/4-inch slices. Place zucchini, broth or stock, dill weed and garlic in a 2-quart saucepan. Bring to a boil, reduce heat and simmer 5 minutes or until zucchini is tender. Remove from heat and cool. Pour mixture into blender or food processor. Add yogurt and evaporated milk and purée. Refrigerate several hours. Serve cold with garnish of fresh zucchini slices or pimiento and parsley. Season to taste with salt and pepper. Makes 6 (1-cup) servings.

Each serving contains:

Cal	Prot	Carb	Fib	Tot. Fat	Sat. Fat	Chol	Sodium
70	7g	10g	1g	0	0	3mg	79mg

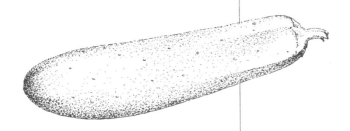

Instant Vichyssoise

Cool and creamy, topped with a sprinkle of chives.

2-1/2 cups chicken broth

1 teaspoon instant minced onion

Prepared instant mashed potatoes for 4 servings

1-1/2 cups evaporated skimmed milk

Chopped chives for garnish

Fresh parsley for garnish

Combine broth and onion in a 2-quart saucepan and heat to boiling. Remove pan from heat and stir in potatoes. Cover; let stand a few minutes to allow potatoes to absorb liquid. Add evaporated milk and pepper, stir well until smooth and creamy. Cover and refrigerate several hours. Serve cold with garnish of chives or fresh parsley. Makes 8 (1/2-cup) servings.

Each serving contains:

Cal	Prot	Carb	Fib	Tot. Fat	Sat. Fat	Chol	Sodium
110	6g	13g	0	4g	1g	3mg	238mg

Chilled Avocado with Crab Soup

Transform these few ingredients into a great starter.

2 large ripe avocados

4-1/2 cups chicken broth

1-1/2 cups evaporated skimmed milk

1 tablespoon lemon juice

1 (6-oz.) pkg. frozen crab meat, thawed and drained

Salt and pepper to taste

Peel, remove pits and chop avocados. In a blender combine avocados with broth, evaporated milk, salt and lemon juice; purée. Reserve a few large pieces of crab meat for garnish. Stir remaining crab into puréed avocado mixture. Refrigerate several hours. Season with salt and pepper to taste. Serve cold. Garnish with reserved crab. Makes 6 (1-cup) servings.

Each serving contains:

Cal	Prot	Carb	Fib	Tot. Fat	Sat. Fat	Chol	Sodium
221	16g	17g	10g	11g	2g	28mg	172mg

Beef Stock

Browning the beef knuckle in the oven assures a deep rich-colored stock.

1 beef knuckle

5 quarts water

6 peppercorns

3 cloves

2 garlic cloves or 1/4 teaspoon garlic powder

1/4 teaspoon anise seed

4 parsnips, cut in 2-inch pieces

1 medium onion, quartered

2 fennel (sweet anise) stalks with leaves or 2 celery stalks

5 sprigs parsley

Salt to taste

Place beef knuckle in a shallow pan. Bake at 400F (205C) until very brown. Remove and place in an 8-quart pot. Add water, peppercorns, cloves, garlic and anise seed. Bring to a full boil, reduce heat and simmer 1-1/2 hours. Add parsnips, onion, fennel or celery and parsley; continue cooking 1-1/2 hours. Cool completely and strain. Salt to taste. Refrigerate stock several hours, then remove congealed fat from surface. Makes 4 to 5 quarts.

Each cup contains:

Cal	Prot	Carb	Fib	Tot. Fat	Sat. Fat	Chol	Sodium
16	3g	0	0	1g	0	1mg	0

Chicken Stock

For convenience, freeze stock in small containers.

1 (3-lb.) chicken, skinned

5 quarts water

6 peppercorns

6 whole cloves

1 large onion with skin, quartered

2 carrots, cut in 2-inch pieces

4 parsnips, cut in 2-inch pieces

2 celery stalks with leaves, cut in 2-inch pieces

4 small turnips, quartered

2 bay leaves

Salt to taste

In an 8-quart pot combine chicken, water, peppercorns and cloves. Cover, bring to a full boil, reduce heat and simmer 1 hour. Remove foam from surface with a small sieve. Add onion, carrots, parsnips, celery, turnips and bay leaves; continue cooking 1-1/2 hours. Remove and discard bay leaves. Cool completely and strain. Salt to taste. Remove chicken from bones and reserve for another use. Refrigerate stock several hours, then remove congealed fat from surface.
Makes 4 to 5 quarts.

Each cup contains:

Cal	Prot	Carb	Fib	Tot. Fat	Sat. Fat	Chol	Sodium
39	5g	1g	0	1g	0	1mg	0

Lamb Stock

Use for Moussaka Soup, page 22.

1-1/2 to 2 lbs. lean lamb: neck or shank meat

4 quarts water

6 peppercorns

2 small garlic cloves, crushed

2 tablespoons dried parsley

1 turnip, quartered

2 carrots, cut in 2-inch pieces

3 parsnips, cut in 2-inch pieces

2 celery stalks, cut in 2-inch pieces

Salt to taste

In an 8-quart pot brown meat well on all sides. Add water, peppercorns, garlic and dried parsley. Bring to a full boil, reduce heat and simmer 1 hour. Add turnip, carrots, parsnips and celery; continue cooking 1-1/2 hours. Cool completely and strain. Salt to taste. Remove meat from bones and reserve for another use. Refrigerate stock several hours, then remove congealed fat from surface. Makes 3-1/2 quarts.

Each cup contains:

Cal	Prot	Carb	Fib	Tot. Fat	Sat. Fat	Chol	Sodium
39	5g	1g	0	1g	0g	1mg	0

Vegetable Stock

This stock has a nice rich brown color, so it's good for replacing beef stock in some recipes.

4 tablespoons margarine

5 medium potatoes, quartered (1-1/2 lbs.)

1 medium yellow onion, quartered

5 carrots, cut in 2-inch pieces

6 parsnips, cut in 2-inch pieces

1 cup chopped fresh parsley with stems

4 quarts water

8 peppercorns

2 bay leaves

1 teaspoon dill seed

Salt to taste

Melt margarine in an 8-quart pot. Add potatoes, onion, carrots, parsnips and parsley; brown well, stirring frequently. Add water, peppercorns, bay leaves and dill seed. Bring to a full boil, reduce heat and simmer covered 1-1/2 hours. Remove and discard bay leaves. Cool completely and strain. Salt to taste. Discard vegetables. Refrigerate stock several hours, then remove congealed fat from surface. Makes 3-1/2 quarts.

Each cup contains:

Cal	Prot	Carb	Fib	Tot. Fat	Sat. Fat	Chol	Sodium
70	2g	12g	2g	2g	0	0	0

Salads

Salads play a variety of roles. They can be served as an appetizer, main dish, side dish or a palate cleanser after the entrée. Whichever you choose, be certain to include at least one per day.

Today there is a wonderful selection of greens to choose from. While they have subtle differences in flavor, they have vibrant color differences. For more robust flavor use romaine or chicory (curly endive), which is even stronger—almost pungent. Do not confuse it with Belgian endive, an almost white, small, slender head, which is described as pleasantly bitter. For added interest include contrasting colors like red leaf lettuce or the beautiful radiccio (Italian chicory) whose white veins contrast the deep-red leaves. Generally these eye-catching ingredients are more expensive, but when used sparingly for special occasions you'll find they are worth it.

Three interesting, rather unattractive beige roots are jícama, Jerusalem artichokes (sunchokes) and celery root (celeriac). Peel away the outer inedible coating and discover a white, crunchy, moist interior. Sliced, cubed or grated, they add interest to any salad.

More familiar roots used in cooking stews and soups—turnip, kohlrabi and rutabaga (swede)—are also delicious in salads. Once again, peel before eating. My parents always raised kohlrabi in our garden. When it was young and tender we enjoyed eating it raw.

Edible flowers such as nasturtium, borage, squash blossoms, pansies, rose petals and pot marigold (calendula) can transform your salad into a spectacular dish.

Garnishing is that extra touch that is noticed and welcomed by all, so save your prettiest sprig of fresh herbs for the place of honor.

Barbecue Bean Salad

A wonderful way to use your leftover beans.

1 bunch fresh spinach or salad mixed greens

1 cup Barbecued Beans, page 104

1 zucchini, sliced

1 tomato, chopped

1/4 lb. jícama, cut in sticks

1 tablespoon lemon juice

1 tablespoon chopped parsley

Rinse spinach or salad greens and pat dry. Line salad plates with spinach or mixed greens. Combine beans with zucchini, tomato, jícama and lemon juice. Divide evenly over spinach, sprinkle with parsley. Makes 6 servings.

Each serving contains:

Cal	Prot	Carb	Fib	Tot. Fat	Sat. Fat	Chol	Sodium
47	2g	10g	2g	0	0	0	35mg

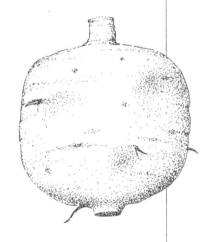

Italian Garbanzo Salad

Prepare this salad any time. I think it's best as a summer lunch.

2 tablespoons canola oil

2 tablespoons sun-dried tomatoes, chopped

1/2 teaspoon dried-leaf oregano

2 tablespoons chopped fresh parsley

2 green onions, chopped

1/2 cup green bell pepper, sliced

1/4 cup lemon juice

1 (15-oz.) can garbanzo beans, rinsed and drained

1-1/2 cups cooked pasta

10 small pimiento-stuffed olives, sliced

1 tomato, chopped

Heat oil, sauté sun-dried tomatoes, oregano, parsley, green onions and green pepper slices. Mix in lemon juice, garbanzo beans, pasta and olives. Stir and toss with tomatoes. Serve warm or chilled. Makes 8 (1/2-cup) servings.

Each serving contains:

Cal	Prot	Carb	Fib	Tot. Fat	Sat. Fat	Chol	Sodium
183	6g	24g	5g	8g	1g	0	123mg

Green Bean-Potato Salad

The Italians inspired my selection of ingredients.

2 cups green beans, cooked

1 cup (1/2 lb.) fresh mushrooms, sliced

2 cups sliced, peeled, cooked potatoes

1/2 cup chopped celery

3 green onions, chopped

1/4 red bell pepper, chopped

1/4 cup raisins

1/4 cup cooked whole-kernel corn

2 tablespoons capers

2 tablespoons pine nuts

1/3 cup Italian Dressing, page 63

In a large salad bowl combine all ingredients. Cover and refrigerate at least 4 hours before serving. Makes 6 (1-cup) servings.

Each serving contains:

Cal	Prot	Carb	Fib	Tot. Fat	Sat. Fat	Chol	Sodium
130	3g	20g	3g	6g	1g	0	18mg

White Bean Salad

Serve in radiccio leaves, they make attractive cups for the salad.

1 (16-oz.) can white kidney beans (cannellini), or 1 cup cooked small white beans, drained

1 (6-oz.) can water-pack tuna, drained

1 cup sliced green bell pepper

1/2 sweet red onion, chopped

2 celery stalks, sliced

1 large tomato, chopped

1 tablespoon chopped fresh parsley

1/2 cup Italian Dressing, page 63

Rinse drained beans with water and drain again. In a salad bowl stir all ingredients together. Cover and chill before serving. Makes 8 servings.

Each serving contains:

Cal	Prot	Carb	Fib	Tot. Fat	Sat. Fat	Chol	Sodium
151	12g	18g	5g	4g	1g	12mg	91mg

Cover Photo

Old-Fashioned Potato Salad

Old-fashioned salad made healthier with yogurt.

3 cups cooked new potatoes

2 tablespoons chopped green olives

1/2 cup cooked peas

1/4 teaspoon dried dill weed

1 tablespoon chopped parsley

1/2 teaspoon sugar

1/4 cup chopped green onions

2 tablespoons lemon juice

2 tablespoons reduced-calorie mayonnaise

1/3 cup nonfat plain yogurt

2 tablespoons chopped chives

1/4 cup chopped celery

Salt and pepper to taste

1 sprig fresh dill for garnish

Slice potatoes and place in a large bowl. Add remaining ingredients; toss gently to combine. Garnish with sprig of fresh dill. Serve either warm or cold. Makes 4 servings.

Each serving contains:

Cal	Prot	Carb	Fib	Tot. Fat	Sat. Fat	Chol	Sodium
148	4g	28g	3g	3g	0g	2mg	236mg

Cover Photo

Confetti Salad

Our colorful picnic slaw.

3 cups shredded red cabbage

1 apple, cored, sliced

1/2 cup dried currants

1/4 cup cooked whole-kernel corn, drained

1/2 cup green grapes

2 celery stalks, sliced

2/3 cup Balsamic Herb Dressing, page 58

In a salad bowl mix cabbage, apple, currants, corn, grapes and celery. Pour Balsamic Herb Dressing over and toss to coat. Makes 6 servings.

Each serving contains:

Cal	Prot	Carb	Fib	Tot. Fat	Sat. Fat	Chol	Sodium
199	2g	21g	3g	14g	2g	0	21mg

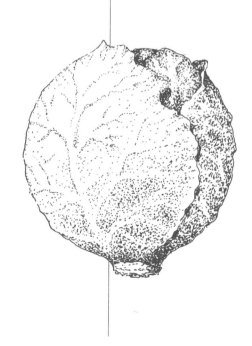

Couscous Fruit Salad

A nice way to introduce couscous, accented with tropical flavors.

1-1/4 cups pineapple-orange juice

1/4 teaspoon cinnamon

1/4 teaspoon mace

1 cup couscous

1 cup pineapple chunks, drained

1 banana, sliced

2 teaspoons lemon juice

1/2 avocado, chopped

3 tablespoons toasted almonds

Place pineapple-orange juice, cinnamon and mace in a saucepan; heat until boiling. Stir in couscous. Cover and remove from heat. Let stand 5 minutes. Spoon in pineapple chunks. Pour mixture into a serving bowl. Top with banana slices. Sprinkle banana slices with lemon juice. Top with avocado and almonds. Makes 6 servings.

Each serving contains:

Cal	Prot	Carb	Fib	Tot. Fat	Sat. Fat	Chol	Sodium
176	4g	30g	4g	5g	1g	0	5mg

Fennel Spinach Salad

A pleasing combination of fresh greens and dried fruits. Fennel is also called Sweet Anise or Finnocio.

1/3 cup chopped dried white figs

1/3 cup chopped dates

1/2 cup Italian Dressing, page 63

1 bunch fresh spinach

1/4 head red-leaf lettuce

1 fennel (sweet anise) bulb, trimmed and sliced

2 tablespoons pine nuts

Place figs and dates in a small bowl, cover with Italian Dressing. Wash spinach, remove stems; pat leaves dry with paper towels. Tear into pieces. Place spinach and fennel slices in a serving bowl. Top with fruits, dressings and pine nuts; toss to combine. Makes 4 servings.

Each serving contains:

Cal	Prot	Carb	Fib	Tot. Fat	Sat. Fat	Chol	Sodium
320	6g	42g	9g	18g	3g	0	77mg

Greek Salad

The Greeks dip their bread into the dressing rather than buttering it.

3 tomatoes, chopped

2 cucumbers, sliced

1/2 green bell pepper, sliced

1/2 onion, chopped

4 radishes, sliced

1 tablespoon capers

1/2 teaspoon dried-leaf oregano

2 tablespoons wine vinegar

4 tablespoons olive oil

1 oz. feta cheese, crumbled

Lettuce leaves, torn in bite-size pieces

12 black Greek olives

In a large bowl combine all ingredients. Chill and serve with a crusty French bread. Makes 4 servings.

Each serving contains:

Cal	Prot	Carb	Fib	Tot. Fat	Sat. Fat	Chol	Sodium
205	3g	13g	4g	17g	3g	6mg	210mg

Island Slaw

The addition of fruit is a nice surprise.

3 tablespoons vinegar

3 tablespoons lemon juice

1/2 teaspoon pepper

3 tablespoons sugar

1 teaspoon caraway seeds

1/4 cup dried currants

1/4 cup chopped dates

1 cup sliced celery

4 cups shredded cabbage

1/2 cup crushed pineapple

In a cup combine vinegar, lemon juice, pepper, sugar, caraway seeds, currants and dates. Let stand 15 minutes. In a large bowl combine remaining ingredients and toss with dressing. Serve at once. Makes 6 servings.

Each serving contains:

Cal	Prot	Carb	Fib	Tot. Fat	Sat. Fat	Chol	Sodium
81	1g	21g	2g	0	0	0	17mg

Mediterranean Salad

A new way to toss a salad and dressing.

1 large tomato, seeded and diced

1 large green pepper, seeded and diced

1 large cucumber, seeded and diced

6 radishes, diced

1 tablespoon chopped Italian parsley

12 small, pitted green olives

2 teaspoons red wine vinegar

1/2 teaspoon black pepper

Bibb lettuce

Combine all vegetables and parsley in bowl. Spray with olive-oil vegetable cooking spray. Mix well. Sprinkle vegetables with vinegar and black pepper. Toss well. Chill about 1 hour. Serve over lettuce leaves. Makes 6 servings.

Each serving contains:

Cal	Prot	Carb	Fib	Tot. Fat	Sat. Fat	Chol	Sodium
25	1g	4g	1g	1g	0	0	192mg

Sunshine Salad

Carrots and orange add a dash of color and flavor to this eye-appealing salad.

1/4 cup vinegar

1/4 cup canola oil

1/3 cup sugar

1 teaspoon dry mustard

1/2 teaspoon celery seed

1 teaspoon grated onion

1/4 teaspoon salt

4 cups shredded red or green cabbage

1 carrot, shredded

1 medium orange, peeled and cut into small chunks

In a small saucepan combine vinegar, oil, sugar, dry mustard, celery seed, onion and salt. Stir over medium heat until sugar dissolves. Cool to room temperature. Combine cabbage, carrot and orange in large bowl. Pour dressing over; toss to coat. Makes 6 to 7 servings.

Each serving contains:

Cal	Prot	Carb	Fib	Tot. Fat	Sat. Fat	Chol	Sodium
129	1g	15g	2g	8g	0	0	87mg

Three-Pepper Salad

Brighten your meal with this great salad.

1/2 cup House Salad Dressing, page 62

1 cup fresh lima beans, cooked

1 red bell pepper, julienned

1 yellow or orange bell pepper, julienned

1 green bell pepper, julienned

2 green onions, chopped

1 cup mushrooms, sliced

1 tablespoon chopped fresh basil or 1 teaspoon dried-leaf basil

Spinach or Romaine lettuce leaves

1 tablespoon toasted pumpkin seeds

Pour House Salad Dressing over lima beans and marinate at least 1 hour. Add remaining ingredients, except spinach leaves and pumpkin seeds, tossing to combine. Line salad bowl with spinach or Romaine lettuce leaves. Place salad on top of leaves. Sprinkle with pumpkin seeds. Makes 4 to 6 servings.

Each serving contains:

Cal	Prot	Carb	Fib	Tot. Fat	Sat. Fat	Chol	Sodium
135	3g	12g	4g	9g	1g	0	21mg

Zucchini Salad

Cucumber can be substituted if zucchini is not available.

1 zucchini, thinly sliced

1 red onion, thinly sliced

2 tomatoes, thinly sliced

3 tablespoons olive oil

1 tablespoon wine vinegar or apple cider

2 tablespoons lemon juice

1/4 teaspoon garlic powder

1/4 teaspoon dill weed

1 tablespoon chopped fresh basil or 1 teaspoon dried-leaf basil

1 tablespoon roasted, unsalted sunflower seeds

In a salad bowl alternate slices of zucchini, red onion and tomatoes. In a cup blend oil, wine vinegar or apple cider, lemon juice, garlic powder, dill weed and basil. Pour over zucchini mixture and sprinkle with sunflower seeds. Cover and chill before serving. Makes 4 to 6 servings.

Each serving contains:

Cal	Prot	Carb	Fib	Tot. Fat	Sat. Fat	Chol	Sodium
90	1g	5g	1g	8g	1g	0	5mg

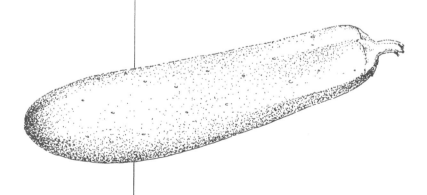

Summer Fruit Salad

A cool satisfying lunch or a special breakfast treat.

1 cantaloupe

1 cup reduced-fat ricotta cheese

1/4 cup orange juice

1 banana, sliced

2 kiwis, sliced, peeled

16 strawberries, halved

Honey Dressing, page 60, or Marmalade Dressing, page 61

Peel melon and cut into slices. Divide them equally on 4 plates. In a small bowl stir cheese and orange juice together. Fold in banana slices. Mound cheese mixture on top of melon slices. Arrange kiwi slices attractively. Garnish with strawberries. Top with Honey or Marmalade Dressing. Makes 4 servings.

Each serving without dressing contains:

Cal	Prot	Carb	Fib	Tot. Fat	Sat. Fat	Chol	Sodium
211	9g	34g	5g	6g	3g	19mg	92mg

Winter Salad

*Grapefruit and apples make a
splendid team.*

Lettuce or spinach leaves

**1 grapefruit, peeled, cut in
segments**

1 apple, cut in eighths

**1/2 cup Marmalade Dressing,
page 61**

1/2 cup green grapes

**2 tablespoons pomegranate
seeds or raspberries**

Arrange lettuce or spinach leaves
on four salad plates. Top with alter-
nating grapefruit segments and
apple slices. Drizzle 2 tablespoons
Marmalade Dressing over each
salad. Top with green grapes and
pomegranate seeds or raspberries.
Makes 4 servings.

Each serving with dressing contains:

Cal	Prot	Carb	Fib	Tot. Fat	Sat. Fat	Chol	Sodium
156	2g	40g	2g	0	0	0	21mg

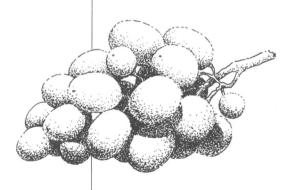

Chicken Salad

A cool, light main-dish salad. Serve with Mediterranean Toast, page 6, and a cold drink.

1 cup cubed, skinned, cooked chicken

1 apple, sliced

1 cucumber, sliced, peeled

1/2 cantaloupe, cubed, peeled

1/2 cup blueberries

1/2 cup green seedless grapes

1/4 head lettuce, torn in bite-size pieces

1/3 cup House Salad Dressing, page 62

Chill all ingredients. Combine all salad ingredients in a large bowl. Toss with dressing. Spoon onto serving plates. Makes 4 servings.

Each serving with white meat contains:

Cal	Prot	Carb	Fib	Tot. Fat	Sat. Fat	Chol	Sodium
207	10g	21g	3g	10g	1g	22mg	44mg

Each serving with dark meat contains:

Cal	Prot	Carb	Fib	Tot. Fat	Sat. Fat	Chol	Sodium
219	9g	21g	3g	12g	1g	25mg	47mg

Shrimp & Scallop Salad

If cantaloupe is not available, substitute papaya or mango slices.

Lettuce or spinach leaves

1 cantaloupe, peeled, sliced

1/2 cup cooked shrimp

1/2 cup cooked scallops

2 celery stalks, sliced

1 green onion, finely chopped

1 cucumber, sliced

12 cherry tomatoes

2 limes or lemons

Line 4 plates with lettuce or spinach leaves. Place 1/4 of cantaloupe slices on each plate. Add a mound of shrimp and scallops, top with celery and green onion. Place cucumbers and cherry tomatoes on the side. Cut limes or lemons into wedges; place on plates. Let each person squeeze wedges over salad as they desire. Makes 4 servings.

Each serving contains:

Cal	Prot	Carb	Fib	Tot. Fat	Sat. Fat	Chol	Sodium
115	9g	19g	4g	1g	0	34mg	94mg

Turkey Melba Salad

Fresh berries make a pretty as well as tasty addition.

1 bunch spinach

1 celery stalk, sliced

1 cup cubed, skinned, cooked turkey

2 fresh peaches, peeled, sliced

1 cup fresh raspberries or strawberries

2 tablespoons toasted pecans

Honey Dressing, page 60, or House Salad Dressing, page 62

Thoroughly rinse spinach. Pat dry and tear into bite-size pieces. In a salad bowl combine spinach, celery, turkey, peaches, raspberries or strawberries and pecans. Toss together gently with Honey or House Salad Dressing.

Or line 6 salad plates with spinach; arrange celery, turkey and peaches on top. Scatter with raspberries or strawberries and top with Honey or House Salad Dressing. Sprinkle with pecans. Makes 6 servings.

Each serving with white meat contains:

Cal	Prot	Carb	Fib	Tot. Fat	Sat. Fat	Chol	Sodium
81	8g	7g	3g	3g	0	16mg	35mg

Each serving with dark meat contains:

Cal	Prot	Carb	Fib	Tot. Fat	Sat. Fat	Chol	Sodium
88	8g	7g	3g	4g	1g	20mg	39mg

Dressings, Relishes & Sauces

Even though a salad or entrée is complete in itself, often the addition of a complementary dressing, relish or sauce adds that special taste which makes it memorable.

I choose a light-flavored oil for most cooking, but will use a more robust olive oil where I feel it enhances the flavor of the dish or dressing. Walnut and avocado oils make wonderful salad dressings.

Enhance a simple vinaigrette by making your own flavored vinegars. This requires some forethought because the best results come after allowing flavors to blend at least three weeks. Experiment with both herb and fruit combinations. A few minutes' preparation can result in giving your dressing that personal touch.

The *Chipotle* chile may be new to you. This brown, plump chile has a distinctive smoky flavor. Canned chipotle chilies are found in the specialty or Mexican food section of your market. Fresh or dried varieties can be purchased in produce markets featuring Hispanic ingredients.

When introducing spicy salsas serve small portions, the combinations can surprise the palate. Flavorful salsas or relishes can accent your broiled chicken, fish or meat entrée. Served as a side dish they brighten any meal, and at our house we enjoy them with sandwiches.

I also offer my own easy uncooked Pineapple Salsa that can be made with other fruits such as papaya, peach, apricot or pear.

The addition of a relish like Taste-of-the-Tropics or Plum Rhubarb Chutney is a delightful way to add more interest to the meal, as well as a bit more fiber.

Balsamic Herb Dressing

Balsamic vinegar gives this simple dressing that special flavor.

3 tablespoons Balsamic vinegar

2 tablespoons lemon juice

6 tablespoons olive oil

3 garlic cloves, crushed

1/2 teaspoon dry mustard

1/2 teaspoon dried-leaf basil

1/2 teaspoon dried-leaf oregano

1/2 teaspoon paprika

Combine all ingredients in a jar with a tight-fitting lid. Or blend ingredients in a food processor or blender. Store in a covered container. Always shake salad dressing vigorously before using. Makes about 2/3 cup.

Each tablespoon contains:

Cal	Prot	Carb	Fib	Tot. Fat	Sat. Fat	Chol	Sodium
68	0	1g	0	7g	1g	0	0

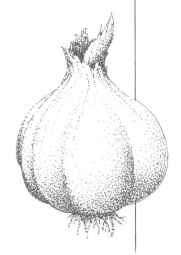

Favorite French Dressing

This was chosen as the favorite dressing for mixed green salads.

1/2 cup canola oil

1/4 cup vinegar

2 tablespoons grated onion

2 tablespoons sugar

1/3 cup catsup

1 teaspoon paprika

1 teaspoon pepper

1 tablespoon lemon juice

1/2 teaspoon prepared Dijon-style mustard

2 garlic cloves

Place all ingredients in blender and mix well. Pour into container and cover. Chill before using. Shake vigorously before pouring on salad greens. Makes about 1-1/4 cups.

Each tablespoon contains:

Cal	Prot	Carb	Fib	Tot. Fat	Sat. Fat	Chol	Sodium
74	0	4g	0	7g	0	0	62mg

Honey Dressing

That extra touch of sweetness for any fruit plate.

1/2 cup honey

1/2 cup lemon juice

3 tablespoons canola oil

Curry powder to taste

Poppy seeds to taste

Combine honey, lemon juice and oil. Add curry powder and poppy seeds to taste. Stir before using. Makes about 1 cup.

Each tablespoon contains:

Cal	Prot	Carb	Fib	Tot. Fat	Sat. Fat	Chol	Sodium
57	0	9g	0	3g	0	0	1mg

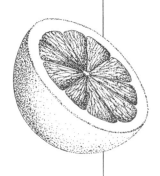

Marmalade Dressing

Fruit salads or green salads taste better when topped with this tangy dressing.

1/2 cup plain nonfat yogurt

2 tablespoons honey

1/4 teaspoon dry mustard

1/2 cup orange, grapefruit or lime marmalade

In a cup stir all ingredients together until thoroughly combined. Cover and refrigerate until ready to use. Stir before using. Makes about 3/4 cups.

Each tablespoon contains:

Cal	Prot	Carb	Fib	Tot. Fat	Sat. Fat	Chol	Sodium
51	1g	13g	0	0	0	0	10mg

House Salad Dressing

Make a double recipe and use half as a marinade for cooked vegetables.

1/3 cup canola oil

1/4 cup cider vinegar

1 teaspoon sugar

1 teaspoon dry mustard

1/2 teaspoon paprika

1/2 teaspoon Worcestershire sauce

1 garlic clove, chopped

Combine all ingredients. Let stand at room temperature at least 2 hours. Stir vigorously before using. Makes about 2/3 cup.

Each tablespoon contains:

Cal	Prot	Carb	Fib	Tot. Fat	Sat. Fat	Chol	Sodium
63	0	1g	0	7g	0	0	11mg

Italian Dressing

Vary the spices to suit your own taste.

1/2 cup olive oil

2 tablespoons cider vinegar

2 tablespoons lemon juice

1 garlic clove

1 green onion, chopped

1/2 teaspoon dried-leaf oregano

1/2 teaspoon dry mustard

2 tablespoons tomato juice

Combine all ingredients in a jar or container with a tight-fitting lid. Shake and let stand an hour before using. Shake vigorously before using. Makes about 1 cup.

Each tablespoon contains:

Cal	Prot	Carb	Fib	Tot. Fat	Sat. Fat	Chol	Sodium
61	0	0	0	7g	1g	0	7mg

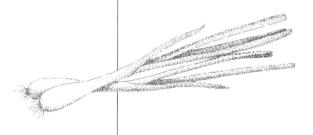

Cucumber-Yogurt Dressing

Make this early in the day and let the flavor develop.

1 cucumber, shredded, peeled, seeded

1/2 cup nonfat plain yogurt

2 tablespoons pine nuts

2 tablespoons capers

1 tablespoon lemon juice

1/2 teaspoon garlic powder

1 tablespoon chopped parsley

Salt and pepper to taste

In a small bowl combine shredded cucumber with remaining ingredients. Cover and chill before serving. Makes about 1-1/4 cups.

Each tablespoon contains:

Cal	Prot	Carb	Fib	Tot. Fat	Sat. Fat	Chol	Sodium
13	1g	1g	0	1g	0	0	5mg

Green-Chile Mayonnaise

Use as a topping on fish or chicken or as a sandwich spread.

1/2 cup reduced-calorie mayonnaise

2 green onions, chopped

3 whole green chiles, seeded

1/4 teaspoon dried-leaf oregano

1 teaspoon lemon juice

Combine all ingredients in a food processor or blender. Process until thoroughly blended. Refrigerate in a container with a tight-fitting lid. Makes about 1 cup.

Each tablespoon contains:

Cal	Prot	Carb	Fib	Tot. Fat	Sat. Fat	Chol	Sodium
21	0	2g	0	1g	0	2mg	38mg

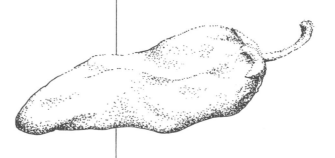

Thousand Island Dressing

Reduced-fat dressing to use with mixed greens or seafood salad.

1/3 cup reduced-calorie mayonnaise

1/3 cup nonfat plain yogurt

3 tablespoons chile sauce or catsup

1 tablespoon minced green pepper

1 teaspoon minced chives

1 teaspoon minced pimiento

2 tablespoons sweet-pickle relish

1/4 teaspoon salt

Pepper to taste

In a small bowl combine mayonnaise, yogurt and chile sauce or catsup. Stir in remaining ingredients. Refrigerate in a container with a tight-fitting lid. Makes about 1 cup.

Each tablespoon contains:

Cal	Prot	Carb	Fib	Tot. Fat	Sat. Fat	Chol	Sodium
20	0	3g	0	1g	0	1mg	118mg

Tomato-Yogurt Sauce

Drained canned tomatoes can be substituted for fresh.

2 large tomatoes, chopped, seeded, peeled

3 tablespoons chopped parsley

1/2 teaspoon Worcestershire sauce

1/2 teaspoon low-sodium soy sauce

1/2 cup nonfat plain yogurt

1 green onion, chopped

In a small bowl combine all ingredients. Cover and refrigerate at least 1 hour for flavors to blend. Makes about 1 cup.

Each tablespoon contains:

Cal	Prot	Carb	Fib	Tot. Fat	Sat. Fat	Chol	Sodium
8	1g	1g	0	0	0	0	25mg

Taste-of-the-Tropics Relish

Especially good with grilled chicken or Barbecued Turkey Burgers, page 237.

1 fresh papaya, diced and peeled

1 (8-oz.) can crushed unsweetened pineapple

1 teaspoon grated orange peel

1/4 teaspoon grated fresh ginger root

1 jalapeño pepper, seeded and finely chopped

2 tablespoons minced green onions

In a small bowl combine papaya, pineapple with juice, orange peel, ginger, jalapeño pepper and green onions. Refrigerate in a container with a tight-fitting lid. Makes about 2 cups.

Each tablespoon contains:

Cal	Prot	Carb	Fib	Tot. Fat	Sat. Fat	Chol	Sodium
8	0	2g	0	0	0	0	4mg

Cran-Apple Sauce

Equally good served as a dessert or as a side dish with poultry or pork.

1 cup fresh cranberries

6 large apples, peeled, cored, and coarsely chopped

1/2 cup sugar

1/3 cup apple juice

1/4 teaspoon ground mace

1/8 teaspoon ground coriander

Combine ingredients in large saucepan. Bring to a boil. Cover and simmer 5 to 10 minutes or until apples are tender. Finely chop in food processor. Cover and refrigerate until cool. Makes about 4 cups.

Each tablespoon contains:

Cal	Prot	Carb	Fib	Tot. Fat	Sat. Fat	Chol	Sodium
14	0	4g	0	0	0	0	0

Sweet & Sour Sauce

Find out how easy it is to make your own sauce.

1 (8-oz.) can pineapple chunks

3/4 cup reserved pineapple juice

1 tablespoon low-sodium soy sauce

1 tablespoon brown sugar

1 tablespoon cider vinegar

2 tablespoons catsup

1 tablespoon cornstarch

1/2 green bell pepper, cut in 1-inch pieces

1 (4-oz.) jar maraschino cherries, drained

Drain juice from pineapple and set pineapple aside. If necessary add water to make 3/4 cup juice. In a saucepan combine juice, soy sauce, brown sugar, vinegar, catsup and cornstarch. Cook, stirring constantly until thickened. Add green pepper, reserved pineapple and cherries. Cook until heated. Serve at once. Makes about 2 cups.

Each tablespoon contains:

Cal	Prot	Carb	Fib	Tot. Fat	Sat. Fat	Chol	Sodium
11	0	3g	0	0	0	0	44mg

Corn-Tomato Sauce

Orange juice adds extra flavor to tomatoes.

4 cups chopped tomatoes

1 onion, chopped

1 green bell pepper, chopped

1 red bell pepper, chopped

1 chile pepper, chopped

1 tablespoon sugar

1/2 teaspoon salt

1/4 teaspoon ginger

1/4 teaspoon nutmeg

1-1/4 cups orange juice

1 (17-oz.) can whole-kernel corn, drained

In a large pot or Dutch oven combine all ingredients except corn. Cook over medium heat about 30 minutes. Stir occasionally. Add corn and cook 5 minutes. Makes about 6 cups.

Each tablespoon contains:

Cal	Prot	Carb	Fib	Tot. Fat	Sat. Fat	Chol	Sodium
90	0	2g	0	0	0	0	24mg

Chipotle Salsa

This smoky-flavored chile from Mexico is gaining popularity.

1 (10-oz.) can chipotle chiles, thinly sliced, drained

1/2 cup water

1/2 cup cider vinegar

2 to 3 tablespoons brown sugar, to taste

1 onion, sliced

Rinse chipotle chiles in water and drain. Remove seeds. In a small bowl combine chiles, water, vinegar, sugar and onion. Cover and refrigerate. This keeps well for 2 weeks. Serve as a condiment. If desired, chop both chiles and onion and use the salsa as a topping on broiled fish or chicken. Makes about 2 cups.

Each tablespoon contains:

Cal	Prot	Carb	Fib	Tot. Fat	Sat. Fat	Chol	Sodium
7	0	2g	0	0	0	0	92mg

Pear & Watermelon Preserve Relish

Accent broiled fish with this tangy mixture.

3 firm, near ripe pears, chopped, cored, peeled

1 (10-oz.) jar watermelon preserves, chopped

1 apple, chopped, cored, peeled

1/2 onion, chopped

2 tablespoons chopped crystallized ginger

3 tablespoons lemon juice

2 tablespoons raisins

3 tablespoons wine vinegar

In a saucepan combine all ingredients. Cover and cook over medium heat about 15 minutes or until pears and apples are tender. Remove from heat. Serve warm or chilled. Makes about 3 cups.

Each tablespoon contains:

Cal	Prot	Carb	Fib	Tot. Fat	Sat. Fat	Chol	Sodium
27	0	7g	0	0	0	0	1mg

Pineapple Salsa

Be daring and substitute papaya, mango, apricot or cantaloupe for the pineapple.

1 roasted whole chile, chopped, seeded, peeled

2 green onions, chopped

2 tablespoons chopped fresh cilantro (Chinese parsley)

1 tablespoon chopped fresh parsley

1 cup fresh or 1 (8-oz.) can pineapple chunks, drained

In a small bowl combine all ingredients. Cover and refrigerate at least 20 minutes before serving. Serve as a topping on broiled fish or chicken or as a relish. Makes about 1-1/2 cups.

Each tablespoon contains:

Cal	Prot	Carb	Fib	Tot. Fat	Sat. Fat	Chol	Sodium
7	0	2g	0	0	0	0	0

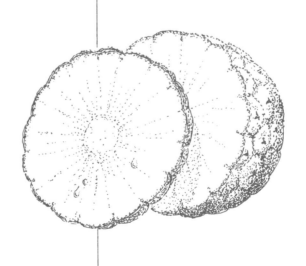

Tomato Salsa

Serve as a dip or topping on Avocado Shrimp Mousse, page 9. Great with any Mexican dish.

1 (8-oz.) can tomato sauce

1/4 cup chopped onion

2/3 cup chopped green chiles

1/4 to 1/2 teaspoon chili powder

2 tomatoes, chopped

1 tablespoon chopped cilantro (Chinese parsley)

Combine all ingredients in a small container. Cover and refrigerate. Let flavor develop 2 to 3 hours before using. Makes about 2 cups.

Each tablespoon contains:

Cal	Prot	Carb	Fib	Tot. Fat	Sat. Fat	Chol	Sodium
6	0	1g	0	0	0	0	44mg

Tomato Marmalade

Tastier than any you could purchase. Use to top any broiled meat or for a sandwich spread.

4 cups peeled tomatoes

4 cups sugar

1/2 teaspoon salt

1/4 cup vinegar

1 small lemon, thinly sliced

1/2 teaspoon ground cinnamon

1/2 teaspoon ground cloves

1/2 teaspoon red (cayenne) pepper

Combine all ingredients in a large pot or Dutch oven. Let stand 20 minutes. Cook over medium heat, stirring occasionally to prevent sticking. Bring to a boil. Cook about 20 minutes. Pour into hot, sterilized jars and seal at once, or let cool and refrigerate. This can be refrigerated for weeks. Makes 4 to 5 (8-oz.) jars.

Each tablespoon contains:

Cal	Prot	Carb	Fib	Tot. Fat	Sat. Fat	Chol	Sodium
82	0	21g	0	0	0	0	29mg

Plum Rhubarb Chutney

Add interest and flavor to grilled meats or fish.

1 lb. rhubarb, cut in 1-inch pieces

1 lb. plums, pitted

1 onion, chopped

1/2 cup pitted chopped dates

1 cup vinegar

1-1/2 cups sugar

1 teaspoon ground ginger

1 teaspoon ground allspice

Combine all ingredients in a large saucepan or Dutch oven. Cook over low heat until mixture becomes jam-like in texture. Cool and spoon into jars. Refrigerate in containers with tight-fitting lids. This keeps under refrigeration for months. Makes about 6 cups.

Each tablespoon contains:

Cal	Prot	Carb	Fib	Tot. Fat	Sat. Fat	Chol	Sodium
19	0	5g	0	0	0	0	0

Breads

Called the *Staff of Life,* bread is what we all include in our diet each day. For many of us the day begins with juice and toast or muffins. It is difficult to think of not enjoying these regularly. You'll find whole grains can be incorporated in many recipes, whether in loaves, rolls, pancakes or muffins.

Quick breads and muffins are gaining in popularity because they are easy to prepare and take little time to bake. Hot muffins can be baking while you prepare the rest of dinner. The little extra effort is always appreciated.

With so many in the work force, many of us no longer have the time required to make yeast breads. But when you have a little extra time, try one of my yeast breads. With a little practice and patience, you'll gain confidence to experiment and personalize the recipes. Simply add your favorite herbs and enjoy.

Pancakes make a wonderful light supper, as well as special breakfast or brunch fare. They are delightfully tender when made with yogurt or cottage cheese. Flavor and interest can be increased by adding your favorite chopped nuts or dried fruit. My Walnut Sweet Potato Pancakes are an example. Try topping them with fresh fruit and powdered sugar or with fruit syrups.

If you enjoy wholesome multi-grain breads but are not inclined to make your own, be selective when shopping. Read the ingredient lists, avoiding products that include whole eggs or undesirable fat. More and more "good-fat" breads are appearing in response to customers' wants and needs.

Buttermilk-Pistachio Pancakes

Tender pancakes with delicious little green nuggets.

1 cup all-purpose flour

2 tablespoons brown sugar

1 tablespoon baking powder

1/2 tablespoon baking soda

1 cup lowfat buttermilk

1 teaspoon vanilla extract

2 tablespoons canola oil

2 egg whites, beaten

3 tablespoons chopped pistachios

Preheat griddle or electric fry pan. Stir together flour, brown sugar, baking powder and baking soda. Beat in buttermilk, vanilla extract, oil and egg whites. Add chopped pistachios. Lightly spray griddle with vegetable cooking spray. Pour 1/4 cup batter for each pancake. Cook 2 to 3 minutes until bubbles appear and surface looks dry. Turn; cook 2 to 3 minutes until browned. Makes 12 (3-inch) pancakes.

Each pancake contains:

Cal	Prot	Carb	Fib	Tot. Fat	Sat. Fat	Chol	Sodium
86	3g	11g	0	4g	0	1mg	216mg

Raisin-Oat Bran Pancakes

Start the day with these raisin treats.

1 cup all-purpose flour

1/2 cup oat bran

1 tablespoon sugar

1 teaspoon baking soda

2 teaspoons baking powder

1/2 teaspoon cinnamon

1/2 cup egg substitute or 4 egg whites, beaten

1-1/2 cups lowfat buttermilk

2 tablespoons canola oil

1/2 teaspoon vanilla extract

1/4 cup raisins

✿ **Variation**
Substitute chopped dates or mixed dried fruit for raisins.

Spray a non-stick griddle with vegetable cooking spray. Preheat griddle. In a bowl stir together flour, oat bran, sugar, baking soda, baking powder and cinnamon. Add egg substitute or beaten egg whites, buttermilk, oil and vanilla; stir to blend. Fold in raisins. Pour about 1/4 cup batter for each pancake. Cook 2 to 3 minutes until bubbles appear and edges look dry. Turn and cook other side 2 to 3 minutes until browned. Makes 18 (3-inch) pancakes.

Each pancake contains:

Cal	Prot	Carb	Fib	Tot. Fat	Sat. Fat	Chol	Sodium
66	3g	11g	1g	2g	0	1mg	118mg

Strawberry Pancakes

These pretty pink pancakes are best when topped with fresh strawberries and powdered sugar.

1 cup all-purpose flour

1/2 teaspoon baking soda

1 teaspoon baking powder

1 cup nonfat strawberry yogurt

2 egg whites

1/3 cup skim milk

1 cup sliced strawberries

Powdered sugar

Preheat griddle. In a bowl stir together flour, baking soda and baking powder. Beat in yogurt, egg whites and skim milk. Spray griddle with vegetable cooking spray. Pour 1/4 cup batter for each pancake. Cook 2 to 3 minutes until bubbles appear and surface looks dry. Turn and cook out side 2 to 3 minutes until lightly browned. Top cooked pancakes with sliced strawberries. Sprinkle with powdered sugar. Makes 12 (3-inch) pancakes.

Each pancake contains:

Cal	Prot	Carb	Fib	Tot. Fat	Sat. Fat	Chol	Sodium
67	3g	13g	1g	0	0	1mg	85mg

Walnut Sweet-Potato Pancakes

Your guests will never guess the unusual ingredients.

1 cup all-purpose flour

2 tablespoons brown sugar

1/2 teaspoon baking soda

1 teaspoon baking powder

1 cup lowfat buttermilk

2 tablespoons canola oil

2 egg whites

1 teaspoon vanilla extract

1/2 cup mashed, cooked sweet potatoes

1/2 teaspoon pumpkin-pie spice

1/4 cup chopped walnuts

Preheat a non-stick griddle or electric fry pan. In a blender or food processor stir flour, brown sugar, baking soda and baking powder together. Add buttermilk, oil, egg whites, vanilla, sweet potatoes, pumpkin-pie spice and combine. Fold in walnuts. Spray griddle with vegetable cooking spray. Pour about 1/4 cup batter for each pancake. Cook 2 to 3 minutes until bubbles appear and edges look dry. Turn and cook other side 2 to 3 minutes until browned. Makes 15 (3-inch) pancakes.

Each pancake contains:

Cal	Prot	Carb	Fib	Tot. Fat	Sat. Fat	Chol	Sodium
79	2g	10g	0	3g	0	1mg	75mg

Chocolate Pecan Waffles

Top with fresh sliced fruit or Apricot Sauce, page 220.

1 cup all-purpose flour

2 tablespoons cocoa

1 teaspoon baking powder

1 tablespoon sugar

3 tablespoons pecans

1 cup lowfat cottage cheese

3 tablespoons canola oil

3 egg whites, beaten

Preheat waffle maker. In a bowl stir together flour, cocoa, baking powder, sugar and pecans. Beat in cottage cheese and oil. Fold in beaten egg whites. Bake according to manufacturer's instructions. Makes about 6 (6-inch) waffles.

Each waffle contains:

Cal	Prot	Carb	Fib	Tot. Fat	Sat. Fat	Chol	Sodium
217	10g	21g	1g	11g	1g	3mg	236mg

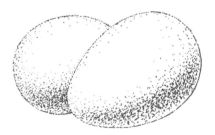

Blue Corn Muffins

Blue cornmeal adds a distinctive flavor and color to these muffins.

2/3 cup blue cornmeal

1-1/3 cups all-purpose flour

1/3 cup sugar

1 tablespoon baking powder

1/4 cup sunflower seeds

2 egg whites, slightly beaten

1/3 cup canola oil

1/2 cup nonfat milk

Preheat oven to 400F (205C). Spray a muffin pan with vegetable cooking spray. In a bowl stir together cornmeal, flour, sugar, baking powder and sunflower seeds. Make a well in center of mixture and pour in egg whites, oil and milk. Stir until dry ingredients are combined. Spoon batter into prepared muffin pan. Bake about 25 minutes or until a wooden pick inserted into center of a muffin comes out clean. Remove from pan; cool 5 minutes and serve. Makes 12 muffins.

Each muffin contains:

Cal	Prot	Carb	Fib	Tot. Fat	Sat. Fat	Chol	Sodium
177	4g	23g	1g	8g	1g	0	97mg

No-Fuss Fig Muffins

Ready to enjoy in minutes.

2 cups buttermilk baking mix

1/2 cup chopped figs

1/4 cup raisins

1/2 cup packed brown sugar

3 tablespoons canola oil

3/4 cup nonfat milk

1/2 teaspoon almond extract

2 egg whites, beaten

Preheat oven to 400F (205C). Line muffin pan cups with paper baking cups or spray with vegetable cooking spray; set aside. In a bowl combine baking mix, figs, raisins and sugar. Make a well in center, pour in oil, milk and almond extract. Gently fold together. Batter will be lumpy. Fold in beaten egg whites. Spoon into prepared muffin cups. Bake 17 to 20 minutes or until a wooden pick inserted into center of a muffin comes out clean. Remove from pan; cool 5 minutes and serve. Makes 12 muffins.

Each muffin contains:

Cal	Prot	Carb	Fib	Tot. Fat	Sat. Fat	Chol	Sodium
188	3g	29g	1g	7g	1g	0	284mg

Orange-Pecan Muffins

A golden-orange interior awaits you.

1-1/2 cups all-purpose flour

1/2 cup rice bran

1 tablespoon baking powder

1/3 cup sugar

1-1/2 teaspoons baking soda

1/4 cup chopped pecans

3 tablespoons canola oil

1 teaspoon vanilla extract

3/4 cup orange juice

1 tablespoon grated orange peel

2 egg whites, beaten

Preheat oven to 400F (205C). Line muffin pan cups with paper baking cups or spray with vegetable cooking spray; set aside. In a bowl stir together flour, bran, baking powder, sugar, baking soda and pecans. In a cup combine oil, vanilla, orange juice and peel. Stir quickly into flour mixture. Fold in beaten egg whites. Spoon into prepared muffin cups. Bake 17 to 20 minutes or until a wooden pick inserted into center of a muffin comes out clean. Remove from pan; cool 5 minutes and serve. Makes 12 muffins.

Each muffin contains:

Cal	Prot	Carb	Fib	Tot. Fat	Sat. Fat	Chol	Sodium
147	3g	22g	2g	6g	1g	0	195mg

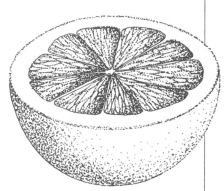

Prune-Bran Muffins

Start your day with fiber-rich, good-tasting muffins.

1/4 cup egg substitute

1 cup lowfat buttermilk

1/3 cup maple syrup

3 tablespoons canola oil

2 cups unprocessed bran

2/3 cup rice bran

1 tablespoon baking powder

1/2 teaspoon ground allspice

1 cup chopped prunes

Preheat oven to 400F (205C). Spray muffin cups with vegetable cooking spray or line with paper baking cups. In a bowl combine egg substitute, buttermilk, maple syrup and oil. Add remaining ingredients. Gently fold together until mixture is moistened; batter will be lumpy. Spoon batter into prepared muffin cups. Bake about 20 minutes or until a wooden pick inserted into center of a muffin comes out clean. Remove from pan; cool 5 minutes and serve. Makes 12 muffins.

Each muffin contains:

Cal	Prot	Carb	Fib	Tot. Fat	Sat. Fat	Chol	Sodium
125	4g	22g	5g	5g	1g	1mg	116mg

Cornmeal Rolls

Warm rolls provide that special touch to any meal.

1/2 cup cornmeal

1-1/2 cups all-purpose flour

1/2 teaspoon salt

2 tablespoons sugar

2 teaspoons baking powder

1/2 teaspoon baking soda

1/4 cup egg substitute

3/4 cup plain lowfat yogurt

Preheat oven to 425F (220C). In a bowl combine cornmeal, flour, salt, sugar, baking powder and baking soda. Add egg substitute and yogurt. Stir together, making a soft dough. Roll out to 1/4 inch. Cut in 2-inch rounds. Fold in half. Bake on ungreased baking sheet 15 minutes or until lightly browned. Makes about 24 rolls.

Each roll contains:

Cal	Prot	Carb	Fib	Tot. Fat	Sat. Fat	Chol	Sodium
50	2g	10g	0	0	0	0	99mg

Lemon-Poppy-Seed Biscuits

Light lemon flavor is a welcome change from the ordinary. If you don't have lemon peel, add 1/2 teaspoon lemon extract.

2 cups all-purpose flour

1 teaspoon grated lemon peel

1 tablespoon baking powder

1-1/2 teaspoons baking soda

1 tablespoon poppy seeds

1 tablespoon sugar

1 cup lowfat lemon-flavored yogurt

1/4 cup nonfat milk

2 tablespoons canola oil

Preheat oven to 450F (230C). In a bowl stir together flour, lemon peel, baking powder, baking soda, poppy seeds and sugar. Combine yogurt, milk and oil. Make a well in center; add yogurt mixture and stir to blend. Turn out onto a lightly floured surface and gently knead 8 to 10 times. Pat dough to 1/2-inch thickness. With a 2-inch biscuit cutter, cut into 12 to 14 biscuits. Or cut into 2-inch squares. Place on ungreased baking sheet. Bake 10 to 12 minutes or until browned. Makes 12 to 14 biscuits.

Each biscuit contains:

Cal	Prot	Carb	Fib	Tot. Fat	Sat. Fat	Chol	Sodium
109	3g	18g	1g	3g	0	1mg	170mg

Date-Pistachio Bread

Rich and chewy, spread slices with Yogurt Cream Cheese, page 3.

1 cup pitted dates, chopped

1/2 cup white grape juice

2/3 cup sugar

1 tablespoon baking powder

1-1/2 cups all-purpose flour

1/2 cup rolled oats

1/2 cup chopped pistachios

1/4 cup canola oil

1/2 teaspoon almond extract

1/4 cup egg substitute or 2 egg whites, beaten

Preheat oven to 350F (175C). Grease a 9 x 5-inch loaf pan; set aside. In a bowl soak dates in grape juice about 5 minutes. Stir in sugar, baking powder, flour, rolled oats, pistachios, oil, almond extract and egg substitute or egg whites. Mix until thoroughly combined. Spoon batter into prepared loaf pan and bake 45 to 50 minutes or until a wooden pick inserted in center comes out clean. Cool in pan 10 minutes; turn out on cooling rack. Makes 1 loaf.

Each slice contains:

Cal	Prot	Carb	Fib	Tot. Fat	Sat. Fat	Chol	Sodium
236	4g	39g	3g	8g	1g	0	95mg

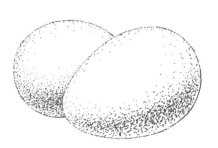

Mango Bread

A wonderful accompaniment to fruit salad.

1-1/2 cups all-purpose flour

1 teaspoon ground cinnamon

1 teaspoon baking soda

1-1/2 teaspoons baking powder

1/4 teaspoon salt

3/4 cup sugar

2 eggs

1/3 cup nonfat milk

3 tablespoons canola oil

1 ripe mango, peeled and chopped

2 tablespoons lemon juice

Preheat oven to 350F (175C). Grease a 9 x 5-inch loaf pan; set aside. In a large bowl combine flour, cinnamon, baking soda, baking powder, salt and sugar. In a medium bowl beat eggs slightly; add milk, oil, mango and lemon juice. Stir into dry ingredients until blended. Pour into prepared pan. Bake in preheated oven about 45 minutes or until a wooden pick inserted in center comes out clean. Cool in pan 10 minutes; turn out on cooling rack. Makes 1 loaf.

Each slice contains:

Cal	Prot	Carb	Fib	Tot. Fat	Sat. Fat	Chol	Sodium
163	3g	28g	1g	4g	1g	36mg	169mg

Carrot-Raisin Loaf

Lemon yogurt combines with carrots for a healthful, yet appetizing bread.

1 cup whole-wheat flour

1 cup all-purpose flour

1 teaspoon baking soda

2 teaspoons baking powder

1/2 teaspoon salt

1/4 teaspoon ground nutmeg

1/2 teaspoon ground cinnamon

2 eggs, beaten slightly

1/3 cup honey

1 cup lowfat lemon yogurt

2 tablespoons canola oil

1/2 cup shredded carrots

1/2 cup chopped raisins

Preheat oven to 325F (165C). Grease a 9 x 5-inch loaf pan; set aside. In a large bowl stir together whole-wheat flour, all-purpose flour, soda, baking powder, salt, nutmeg and cinnamon. In a medium bowl combine eggs, honey, yogurt and oil. Add to dry mixture. Stir until well blended. Stir in carrots and raisins. Bake in preheated oven 45 to 50 minutes or until a wooden pick inserted in center comes out clean. Cool in pan 10 minutes. Turn out on cooling rack. Makes 1 loaf.

Each slice contains:

Cal	Prot	Carb	Fib	Tot. Fat	Sat. Fat	Chol	Sodium
173	5g	32g	2g	4g	1g	36mg	236mg

Prune-Banana Bread

Prunes add extra flavor and moisture to banana bread.

1/3 cup margarine

1 cup sugar

1/2 cup egg substitute or 4 egg whites

1 cup mashed bananas

1-2/3 cup all-purpose flour

1/3 cup oat bran

1 teaspoon baking soda

1 teaspoon vanilla extract

1/2 cup chopped, pitted prunes

Preheat oven to 350F (175C). Grease a 9 x 5-inch loaf pan; set aside. In a mixer bowl beat together margarine and sugar. Beat in egg substitute or egg whites and mashed bananas. Gradually mix in flour, oat bran and baking soda. Stir in vanilla extract and prunes. Spoon batter into prepared loaf pan. Bake about 1 hour or until a wooden pick inserted in center comes out clean. Let cool 10 minutes before removing from pan. Cool before slicing. Makes 1 loaf.

Each slice contains:

Cal	Prot	Carb	Fib	Tot. Fat	Sat. Fat	Chol	Sodium
202	4g	39g	2g	5g	1g	0	152mg

Oatmeal Herb Yeast Bread

Toast slices for the best tasting sandwiches you've ever eaten.

1/4 cup olive oil

2 tablespoons brown sugar

1 cup warm milk

1/2 teaspoon salt

1/2 teaspoon dried-leaf basil

1/2 teaspoon caraway seeds

1/2 teaspoon dried-leaf tarragon

1 (1/4-oz.) pkg. dry yeast

1-1/2 cup rolled oats

2-1/2 cups all-purpose flour

In a mixer bowl combine oil, brown sugar, milk, salt, basil, caraway seeds, tarragon leaves and yeast. Let stand about 5 minutes. With mixer running, blend in oats and one-half flour. Turn dough out on lightly floured surface and knead in remaining flour. Place dough in a lightly oiled bowl, cover and let rise until double in bulk. Turn dough out, punch down and form in loaf; preheat oven to 375F (190C). Place in a greased 9 x 5-inch pan. Bake 35 to 40 minutes until golden brown and loaf sounds hollow when tapped. Remove from pan and cool. Makes 1 loaf.

Each slice contains:

Cal	Prot	Carb	Fib	Tot. Fat	Sat. Fat	Chol	Sodium
191	5g	30g	2g	5g	1g	0	102mg

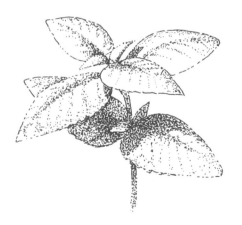

Honey Sunflower Bread

Homemade bread combines goodness and flavor.

1/3 cup honey

2 cups hot water

2 tablespoons margarine

2 tablespoons sunflower seeds

1 cup rolled oats

1 (1/4-oz.) pkg. active dry yeast

1/4 cup warm water

4-1/2 to 5 cups all-purpose flour

In a mixer bowl stir together honey, hot water, margarine and sunflower seeds. Stir in oats. Set aside for 15 to 20 minutes. In a cup stir yeast in warm water, let stand 5 minutes; add to oat mixture. Use a dough hook to beat in about 4 cups flour. Mix thoroughly. Turn out on a lightly floured board. Gently knead adding more flour as necessary. Place dough in a large oiled bowl, turning dough to coat top. Cover; let rise about 1-1/2 hours until doubled in bulk. Punch down dough. Shape into 2 loaves. Place in two greased 9 x 5-inch pans. Let rise again. Preheat oven to 375F (190C). Bake about 50 minutes until loaves sound hollow when tapped. Remove from pan and cool. Makes 2 loaves.

Each slice contains:

Cal	Prot	Carb	Fib	Tot. Fat	Sat. Fat	Chol	Sodium
124	3g	24g	1g	2g	0	0	13mg

Basic Pizza Dough

Use your favorite topping, or try our
Tomato-Onion Topping, page 98.

1 (1/4-oz.) pkg. active dry yeast

1 cup warm water

1 tablespoon olive oil

1/2 teaspoon salt

2 teaspoons finely chopped onion

3 cups all-purpose flour

In a mixer bowl dissolve yeast in warm water. Add oil, salt, chopped onion and 1-1/2 cups flour. Beat until thoroughly combined, making a soft dough. Turn dough out onto a floured surface. Knead in enough flour to make a stiff dough. Spray a bowl with olive oil cooking spray. Place dough in bowl, cover and let rise until doubled in bulk. Punch down dough; cut in half and roll out to fit two 12-inch pans. Makes 2 (12-inch) pizzas.

Each 2-inch slice contains:

Cal	Prot	Carb	Fib	Tot. Fat	Sat. Fat	Chol	Sodium
125	3g	24g	1g	1g	0	0	90mg

Tomato-Onion Topping

Pizza is great without the cheese, or use this topping on toasted French bread or English muffins.

Basic Pizza Dough, page 97

1 tablespoon olive oil

2 onions, sliced

3 tomatoes, thinly sliced

1/4 cup sliced black olives

Basil to taste

Oregano to taste

Pepper to taste

1 tablespoon olive oil

Prepare Pizza Dough. Preheat oven to 425F (220C). In a large skillet heat olive oil. Add onions and sauté briefly. Arrange onion slices on top of pizza dough. Top with sliced tomatoes and olives. Sprinkle with basil, oregano and pepper to taste. Drizzle with olive oil. Bake 15 to 20 minutes until browned. Makes topping for two (12-inch) pizzas.

Topping for each 2-inch slice contains:

Cal	Prot	Carb	Fib	Tot. Fat	Sat. Fat	Chol	Sodium
18	0	2g	0	1g	0	0	12mg

Beans, Rice & Pasta

Nutritionists are encouraging us to increase our grain consumption. Grains provide vitamins, minerals, protein and fiber needed to maintain a balanced diet.

Before preparing beans, rinse them in water and remove any debris or broken beans. Presoak beans to shorten cooking time. There are two basic methods of presoaking. The first is to place the beans in a large bowl or pan that will accommodate at least double the amount of beans. Pour water to cover beans about 2 to 3 inches, keep covered and soak 8 hours. Or place beans in a pot and cover with water; bring to a boil and cook 2 minutes in rapidly boiling water. Cover, remove from heat and let stand about 1 hour. Drain water and replace with fresh water. Proceed to cook. When using canned beans, rinse with water and drain, thus reducing the sodium.

It is easy to work grains into your diet with just a little thought. Try Golden Rice, Confetti Grits or Barley Skillet Dinner. For a change try some of the less-familiar grains like millet and quinoa. These have been eaten for centuries by people in other countries.

Pasta is climbing to the top of preferred foods. We're told Marco Polo brought pasta from China to Italy. I for one will always be grateful! It's versatile as well as nutritious and combines easily with other foods. It's delicious served hot or cold. Pasta made from semolina is still the most popular. However for variety, try other flavors like spinach, beet, carrot, tomato and whole wheat.

Making your own pasta is easy, especially with the wonderful pasta machines that roll and cut the dough for you. Fresh pasta, unlike dried, cooks very quickly. Overcooking will result in a gummy mess.

Fruited Brown Rice

Dried and fresh fruits combine nicely with the nutty flavor of brown rice.

2 cups cooked brown rice

2 tablespoons toasted almonds

4 dried figs, chopped

1 celery stalk, chopped

1 cup seedless red grapes

1/2 cup lowfat orange yogurt

1/4 cup orange juice

1 orange, chopped, peeled, or 1 (11-oz.) can mandarin oranges, drained

1 tablespoon fresh mint, if desired

In a large bowl toss together rice, almonds, figs, celery and grapes. In a cup stir together orange yogurt and orange juice. Pour over rice mixture and stir to combine. Garnish with chopped oranges and fresh mint if desired. Cover and refrigerate until chilled. Makes 6 servings.

Each serving contains:

Cal	Prot	Carb	Fib	Tot. Fat	Sat. Fat	Chol	Sodium
165	4g	34g	4g	2g	0	1mg	22mg

Golden Rice

Delicious as a side dish, try it with a dollop of Green-Chile Mayonnaise, page 65, or plain yogurt.

2 cups chicken broth

1 cup uncooked long-grain white rice

3/4 teaspoon turmeric

2 green onions, chopped

1/4 cup chopped pistachios

1 (11-oz.) can mandarin oranges, drained

In a saucepan bring chicken broth to a boil. Stir in rice and turmeric. Cover and reduce heat to simmer. Cook about 20 minutes. Stir in green onions, pistachios and mandarin orange segments. Gently toss with a fork to combine. Serve hot or cold. Makes 6 servings.

Each serving contains:

Cal	Prot	Carb	Fib	Tot. Fat	Sat. Fat	Chol	Sodium
189	5g	35g	2g	3g	1g	0	5mg

Mexican Rice

*Olé, serve with Soft Chicken Tacos,
page 191.*

**1 cup uncooked long-grain
white rice**

**3/4 cup chopped green bell
pepper**

1 cup chopped onion

1/4 cup diced celery

**2 tablespoons chopped mild
green chiles**

1 garlic clove, minced

2 tomatoes, peeled, chopped

1/4 cup frozen peas

2 cups chicken broth

1/2 teaspoon dried-leaf oregano

1/2 teaspoon black pepper

1/2 teaspoon chili powder

Spray a large skillet with olive oil
vegetable cooking spray; heat over
medium heat. Add rice and sauté
briefly; do not brown. Remove rice
to bowl. In the same skillet sauté
green peppers, onion, celery, chiles
and garlic until onion is golden
brown. Add tomatoes and peas.
Return rice to skillet. Add chicken
broth to rice along with black pepper, oregano and chili powder.
Cover, reduce heat to low and simmer 20 to 25 minutes or until broth
is absorbed. Fluff mixture with a
fork before serving. Makes
4 servings.

Each serving contains:

Cal	Prot	Carb	Fib	Tot. Fat	Sat. Fat	Chol	Sodium
235	8g	48g	3g	1g	0	1mg	30mg

Pilaf

Currants and pine nuts add extra crunch to a traditional side dish.

2 teaspoons olive oil

1 onion, chopped

1/4 cup dried currants or chopped raisins

1/4 cup pine nuts

1/2 teaspoon pumpkin-pie spice

1 cup rice

1 cup vermicelli, broken in 1-inch pieces

2-1/4 cups chicken broth

Heat oil, sauté onion. Add remaining ingredients. Bring to a boil; reduce heat. Cover and cook about 20 minutes until rice is tender and liquid is absorbed. Fluff mixture with a fork before serving. Makes 6 servings.

Each serving contains:

Cal	Prot	Carb	Fib	Tot. Fat	Sat. Fat	Chol	Sodium
257	8g	46g	2g	5g	1g	0	4mg

✿ **Variation**
Pilaf Casserole

Add 1/2 cup chopped carrots and 1 cup cooked chopped chicken.

Barbecued Beans

Serve with Sunshine Salad, page 49, and corn bread for a well-balanced meal.

1/4 lb. Canadian bacon, cubed

1 onion, chopped

1-1/2 teaspoons dry mustard

1 cup coffee

1/4 cup lemon juice or vinegar

1/4 cup tomato paste

3/4 cup water

1/2 teaspoon paprika

1/2 teaspoon chili powder

1/2 cup packed brown sugar

2 cups cooked small white beans

Spray a non-stick skillet with vegetable cooking spray. Sauté bacon and onion. Pour all ingredients in a 2-quart baking dish or bean pot. Stir to combine ingredients. Bake uncovered in 350F (175C) oven about 1 hour. Makes 8 (1-cup) servings.

Each serving contains:

Cal	Prot	Carb	Fib	Tot. Fat	Sat. Fat	Chol	Sodium
154	8g	29g	4g	1g	0	7mg	214mg

Boston Beans

Aunt Helen claims this to be the best of the baked beans.

1 lb. navy or small white beans

1-1/2 cups packed brown sugar

1/2 cup molasses

1 large onion, chopped

1/2 cup catsup

1 tablespoon Worcestershire sauce

1 tablespoon maple syrup

1 teaspoon dry mustard

Salt and pepper to taste

Rinse beans, place in a large pot and cover with water. Bring to a boil, reduce heat; cover and simmer about 1-1/2 hours. Add more water as needed to keep beans covered. Drain beans. Discard liquid. Place beans in a 3-quart casserole or bean pot; add remaining ingredients and stir. Bake at 300F (150C) about 2 hours. If needed, add hot water to keep beans covered. Makes 8 servings.

Each serving contains:

Cal	Prot	Carb	Fib	Tot. Fat	Sat. Fat	Chol	Sodium
309	6g	74g	6g	0	0	0	291mg

Lima Bake

A hearty winter meal. Serve with a crusty French bread and Confetti Slaw, page 43.

2 cups large dried lima beans

1 cup packed brown sugar

2/3 cup molasses

2 tablespoons horseradish

1/4 lb. Canadian bacon, cubed

Salt and pepper to taste

Rinse beans. Place in a large pot; cover with water. Bring to a boil and cook 2 minutes. Cover and remove from heat. Set aside about 1 hour. Drain liquid and add fresh water to cover by 3 inches. Bring to a boil; reduce heat and simmer until tender about 1 to 1-1/2 hours. Add more water if necessary to keep beans covered. In a 2-quart casserole combine beans with remaining ingredients. Bake in 325F (165C) oven about 1 hour until tender. Season to taste with salt and pepper. Makes 8 servings.

Each serving contains:

Cal	Prot	Carb	Fib	Tot. Fat	Sat. Fat	Chol	Sodium
334	13g	70g	14g	1g	0	7mg	226mg

Stove-Top Beans

Ready in minutes to accompany grilled chicken.

2 (16-oz.) cans small white or pinto beans, drained

1 teaspoon canola oil

1 garlic clove, minced

1/4 onion, chopped

1 teaspoon dry mustard

1 (8-oz.) can pineapple chunks in unsweetened juice

Rinse beans and drain again. Set aside. Heat oil in a saucepan. Sauté garlic and onion. Add remaining ingredients, simmer about 10 minutes. Makes 4 servings.

Each serving contains:

Cal	Prot	Carb	Fib	Tot. Fat	Sat. Fat	Chol	Sodium
370	21g	69g	19g	3g	0	0	6mg

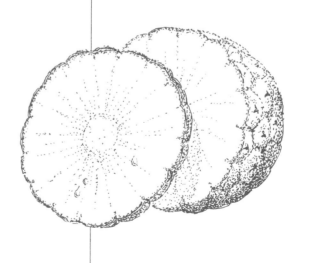

White Bean & Wine Bake

Serve this unusual bean dish with Chicken in Salsa Verde, page 190.

4 cups cooked white beans, drained

1 onion, sliced

1 cup chicken broth

1 cup white wine

1/2 teaspoon chile-pepper flakes

1 tablespoon chopped cilantro (Chinese parsley)

2 tablespoons lemon peel

1/2 teaspoon paprika

Salt and pepper to taste

Preheat oven to 350F (175C). In a baking dish combine all ingredients. Cover and bake 40 minutes. Uncover and bake 15 minutes longer. Makes 4 servings.

Each serving contains:

Cal	Prot	Carb	Fib	Tot. Fat	Sat. Fat	Chol	Sodium
316	18g	50g	15g	2g	0	0	8mg

Barley Casserole

This will help to cultivate a taste for barley.

2 teaspoons olive oil

1 onion, chopped

2 tablespoons chopped fresh parsley

1 cup sliced mushrooms

1 cup barley

2 cups chicken broth

1/4 cup white wine

1/2 teaspoon thyme

1 teaspoon curry powder

1 (6 oz.) pkg. frozen pea pods, thawed

Salt and pepper to taste

Preheat oven to 350F (175C). Heat oil in a medium baking pan; carefully remove from oven and add onions, parsley, mushrooms and barley. Stir to coat. Add wine, thyme and curry powder. Cover and bake about 45 minutes. Uncover, stir in peas; return to oven 7 to 10 minutes. Makes 8 (1/2-cup) servings.

Each serving contains:

Cal	Prot	Carb	Fib	Tot. Fat	Sat. Fat	Chol	Sodium
126	5g	21g	6g	2g	0	0	5mg

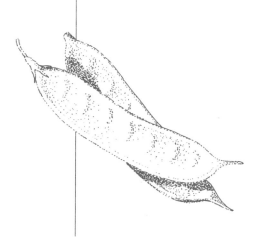

Barley Skillet Dinner

Because it has a short growing season, barley is grown from the Arctic shores to sub-tropical climates.

1 tablespoon canola oil

1 onion, chopped

2 celery stalks, sliced

2 carrots, sliced

3 cups chicken broth

3 tablespoons lemon juice

3/4 cup quick-cooking barley

1 (10-oz.) pkg. frozen or 3/4 lb. fresh Brussels sprouts

1 cup cubed, cooked chicken

Salt and pepper to taste

2 tablespoons grated Romano cheese

In a large skillet or Dutch oven heat oil. Sauté onion, celery and carrots. Add broth and lemon juice; stir in barley. Cover, reduce heat to simmer and cook about 25 minutes. Add Brussels sprouts and chicken. Cover and cook about 10 minutes until sprouts are tender and liquid is absorbed. Season to taste with salt and pepper. Sprinkle with cheese. Serve at once. Makes 6 servings.

Each serving with white meat contains:

Cal	Prot	Carb	Fib	Tot. Fat	Sat. Fat	Chol	Sodium
150	12g	17g	5g	5g	1g	17mg	70mg

Each serving with dark meat contains:

Cal	Prot	Carb	Fib	Tot. Fat	Sat. Fat	Chol	Sodium
158	11g	17g	5g	6g	1g	19mg	73mg

Lasagne

Your guests will ask for seconds.

1/2 cup dried mushrooms

1 cup hot water

8 oz. sweet Italian sausage links

1 teaspoon olive oil

1 onion, chopped

2 carrots, sliced

1 celery stalk, sliced

1 (16-oz.) can whole tomatoes

1-1/2 teaspoons Italian seasoning

1 cup dry red wine or tomato juice

1 (8-oz.) pkg. spinach lasagne

1 cup reduced-fat ricotta cheese

1/2 cup Yogurt Cream Cheese, page 3

4 oz. mozzarella cheese, thinly sliced

1/4 cup grated Parmesan cheese

Soak mushrooms in hot water about 15 minutes. Remove mushrooms and slice, reserve soaking water. Remove sausage from casing, cook sausage in a large saucepan until browned, drain excess fat. Add oil and sauté onion, carrots and celery. Add tomatoes, Italian seasoning, wine or tomato juice and reserved mushroom soaking water. Reduce heat and simmer uncovered about 45 minutes. Cook lasagne according to package instructions. Drain and set aside. Spray a 13 x 9-inch baking dish with olive-oil vegetable cooking spray. Combine ricotta and cream cheese. Alternate layers of lasagne, tomato mixture, ricotta mixture and slices of mozzarella. Sprinkle top with Parmesan cheese. Cover and bake at 350F (175C) 30 minutes. Uncover and cook 12 to 15 minutes until top is lightly browned. Makes 15 servings.

Each serving contains:

Cal	Prot	Carb	Fib	Tot. Fat	Sat. Fat	Chol	Sodium
173	9g	19g	3g	6g	3g	16mg	220mg

Quick & Easy Spaghetti

Amazingly simple; tastes like you've spent hours creating this sauce.

1 lb. sweet Italian sausage links

1/4 onion, chopped

1 (28-oz.) can whole tomatoes, chopped

1-1/2 teaspoons Italian seasoning

1 (8-oz.) can tomato sauce

Cooked spaghetti

Fresh chopped parsley

Slit sausage open and remove casing; crumble or slice sausage. In a skillet brown sausages, drain excess fat. Add onion and sauté. Add tomatoes with juice and Italian seasoning. Cover and cook about 20 minutes. Add tomato sauce, cook 5 minutes longer. Serve over spaghetti. Sprinkle with chopped parsley. Makes 6 servings.

Each serving contains:

Cal	Prot	Carb	Fib	Tot. Fat	Sat. Fat	Chol	Sodium
162	9g	10g	2g	10g	3g	29mg	792mg

Pasta Primavera

Serve warm or chilled. Dinner is ready in 30 minutes.

1/2 lb. or 1 medium head broccoli, coarsely chopped

3 asparagus spears, cut in 2-inch pieces

1 zucchini, halved lengthwise and sliced

1 yellow pepper, sliced

2 garlic cloves, minced

1/4 cup fresh parsley

1/4 cup chicken broth

2 tablespoons dried-leaf basil

1 teaspoon dried-leaf oregano

1 (16-oz.) pkg. pasta

12 cherry tomatoes, halved

Salt and pepper to taste

Spray a large skillet with olive-oil vegetable cooking spray. Add broccoli, asparagus, zucchini, yellow pepper and garlic and sauté 5 to 7 minutes. Set aside. Combine parsley, chicken broth, basil and oregano in blender or food processor. Blend until parsley is fine and moist. Cook pasta according to package directions. Add parsley mixture and tomatoes and toss. Add sautéed vegetables and toss. Season with salt and pepper to taste. Serve warm or chilled. Makes 8 servings.

Each serving contains:

Cal	Prot	Carb	Fib	Tot. Fat	Sat. Fat	Chol	Sodium
237	9g	48g	4g	1g	0	0	17mg

Pasta with Vegetable Sauce

Turn the bounty of a garden into a light meal.

1 tablespoon olive oil

1 onion, sliced

2 garlic cloves, minced

1 fennel (sweet anise) bulb, sliced

1 green pepper, sliced

1 red pepper, sliced

1 yellow pepper, sliced

1 cup sliced mushrooms

2 tomatoes, chopped

3/4 cup tomato juice

1/2 teaspoon dried-leaf thyme

1/2 teaspoon dried-leaf basil

1 tablespoon chopped fresh parsley

Cooked macaroni

Grated Parmesan cheese

In a large skillet or Dutch oven heat oil. Sauté onion and garlic. Add remaining ingredients. Stir and cook over medium heat until vegetables are tender. Serve over cooked pasta. Sprinkle each serving with grated cheese. Makes 6 servings.

Each serving contains:

Cal	Prot	Carb	Fib	Tot. Fat	Sat. Fat	Chol	Sodium
58	2g	9g	2g	3g	0	0	128mg

Fettuccine with Herbs and Walnuts

An ideal light lunch or side dish.

1/2 lb. fettuccine

3 tablespoons olive oil

1 tablespoon margarine

1/4 cup minced parsley

2 teaspoons dried-leaf oregano

2 teaspoon dried-leaf basil

1 teaspoon dried-leaf rosemary

2 garlic cloves, minced

3 tablespoons toasted walnuts

2 tablespoons grated Parmesan cheese

Cook fettuccine according to package directions. Cover, set aside. In a small skillet heat oil, margarine, parsley, oregano, basil, rosemary and garlic. Cook over low heat about 2 minutes. Remove from heat; set aside. In a large serving dish, combine warm fettuccine, herb mixture, walnuts and Parmesan cheese. Toss gently to combine. Serve at once. Makes 4 servings

Each serving contains:

Cal	Prot	Carb	Fib	Tot. Fat	Sat. Fat	Chol	Sodium
375	10g	45g	3g	17g	3g	2mg	89mg

Zucchini and Pasta in Tomato Sauce

Tender fresh zucchini in a simple sauce.

1 tablespoon olive oil

1/2 large onion, chopped

2 large garlic cloves, minced

1/4 cup chopped Italian parsley

1 teaspoon dried-leaf basil

1/4 teaspoon dried-leaf oregano

1 (28-oz.) can Italian peeled tomatoes

1/4 cup red wine

1/4 cup tomato paste

1/2 cup water

1/2 lb. pasta

1 lb. zucchini, sliced

3 tablespoons grated Parmesan cheese

Salt and pepper to taste

Spray a large skillet with vegetable cooking spray. In prepared skillet heat oil; add onion, garlic, parsley, basil and oregano. Sauté 2 to 3 minutes until onion is soft. Add tomatoes and juice, wine, tomato paste and water. Cover, reduce heat to low and simmer 15 to 20 minutes. Meanwhile, cook pasta according to package directions, omitting salt. Add zucchini to tomato sauce, cover and simmer 10 to 15 minutes or until zucchini is tender. In a large bowl combine tomato sauce and pasta. Sprinkle with cheese and season with salt and pepper to taste. Makes 6 servings.

Each serving contains:

Cal	Prot	Carb	Fib	Tot. Fat	Sat. Fat	Chol	Sodium
233	9g	40g	5g	4g	1g	2mg	276mg

Zucchini-Stuffed Shells

Jumbo shells provide an interesting way to enhance zucchini for a main dish.

3 medium zucchini, shredded

1/2 teaspoon salt

12 jumbo pasta shells

2 tablespoons canola oil

3 egg whites, beaten slightly

1 tablespoon chopped chives

1/2 cup reduced-fat ricotta cheese

3/4 cup soft bread crumbs

1/8 teaspoon pepper

3/4 teaspoon fines herbs

3 tablespoons margarine

3 tablespoons all-purpose flour

1-1/2 cups nonfat milk

1-1/2 teaspoons chicken bouillon granules

3/4 teaspoon Worcestershire sauce

1/3 cup shredded Monterey Jack cheese

Sprinkle zucchini with 1/2 teaspoon salt; drain in colander about 15 minutes. Cook pasta according to package directions; drain and toss with oil. With back of spoon, press excess liquid out of zucchini. In a medium bowl combine zucchini with egg whites, chives, ricotta, bread crumbs, pepper and fines herbs. Spoon into cooked shells. Place in shallow baking dish. Preheat oven to 350F (175C). In a medium saucepan melt margarine; stir in flour. Cook and stir until mixture is light golden in color. Add milk, bouillon granules and Worcestershire sauce. Cook until thickened. Spoon over filled shells; sprinkle with cheese. Heat about 20 minutes in preheated oven or until bubbly. Makes 12 shells.

Each shell contains:

Cal	Prot	Carb	Fib	Tot. Fat	Sat. Fat	Chol	Sodium
206	8g	27g	2g	7g	2g	6mg	376mg

Oriental Noodles and Broccoli

Peanuts enhance foods across the world from Africa, Mexico and the Orient.

1 lb. fresh or frozen rice noodles

1 (10-oz.) pkg. frozen or 3/4 lb. fresh cooked broccoli spears

2 tablespoons smooth-style peanut butter

1/2 cup orange juice

1/4 teaspoon ground nutmeg

2 mild or jalapeño chiles, chopped

1 tablespoon low-sodium soy sauce

2 green onions, chopped

1 teaspoon five-spice powder

1 papaya, sliced, peeled, seeded

2 teaspoons chopped dry-roasted peanuts

1 teaspoon toasted sesame seeds

Cook noodles according to package directions. Drain, place in a serving dish. Top with cooked broccoli. Cover and refrigerate. In a food processor or blender combine peanut butter, orange juice, nutmeg, chiles, soy sauce, green onions and five-spice powder. Pour sauce over chilled noodles and broccoli. Top with papaya slices, peanuts and sesame seeds. Makes 4 servings.

Each serving contains:

Cal	Prot	Carb	Fib	Tot. Fat	Sat. Fat	Chol	Sodium
562	22g	105g	13g	8g	2g	0	364mg

Confetti Grits

Grits are pleasantly disguised by south-of-the-border flavors.

3 cups Chicken Stock, page 34, or broth

1/4 teaspoon salt

3/4 cup quick hominy grits

1 (4-oz.) can diced green chiles, drained

1 medium tomato, peeled, seeded and chopped

1 tablespoon chopped cilantro (Chinese parsley)

1 tablespoon minced green onion

1/4 cup shredded Monterey Jack cheese

Heat chicken stock and salt to boiling. Gradually add grits. Cook and stir over medium heat until thickened. Stir in chiles, tomato, cilantro and green onions. Stir in cheese. Makes 6 servings.

Each serving contains:

Cal	Prot	Carb	Fib	Tot. Fat	Sat. Fat	Chol	Sodium
55	4g	5g	1g	2g	1g	5mg	117mg

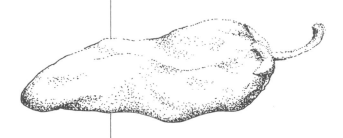

Quinoa Casserole

Pronounced KEEN WAH, this nutritious grain is gaining in availability and popularity.

1/2 cup quinoa

1 cup chicken broth

1/4 teaspoon turmeric

1 tablespoon lemon juice

1/2 cup chopped dates

1 cup cubed, cooked chicken

1/2 cup frozen peas

1/4 red or yellow bell pepper, chopped

2 tablespoons chopped dry roasted peanuts

Thoroughly rinse quinoa several times in water. Drain. Pour chicken broth and turmeric in a saucepan, add quinoa; bring to a boil. Cover, reduce heat and simmer about 15 minutes until broth is absorbed. Add remaining ingredients and cook until heated. Makes 4 servings.

Each serving with white meat contains:

Cal	Prot	Carb	Fib	Tot. Fat	Sat. Fat	Chol	Sodium
222	14g	35g	4g	4g	1g	22mg	41mg

Each serving with dark meat contains:

Cal	Prot	Carb	Fib	Tot. Fat	Sat. Fat	Chol	Sodium
234	12g	35g	4g	6g	1g	25mg	44mg

Lentils
with Vegetables

Extra spice adds zest to this hearty dish.

1 cup dried lentils

1/2 onion, chopped

1/2 teaspoon cardamom

1 carrot, sliced

1/2 teaspoon pepper

1 red bell pepper, sliced

1/2 teaspoon ground cinnamon

2 cups Vegetable Stock, page 36, or water

1 (16-oz.) can tomatoes

Salt to taste

Rinse and sort lentils. In a saucepan or Dutch oven combine all ingredients. Bring to a boil. Cover, reduce heat and simmer about 30 minutes until lentils are done. Season to taste with salt. Makes 6 servings.

Each serving contains:

Cal	Prot	Carb	Fib	Tot. Fat	Sat. Fat	Chol	Sodium
161	11g	29g	6g	1g	0	0	131mg

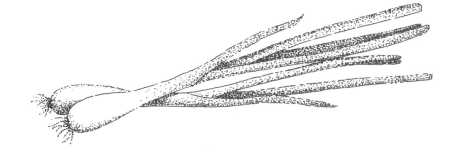

Vegetables

It is difficult to imagine what our meals would be without vegetables. They provide nutrition, color, texture and flavor. Rapid shipping allows us to enjoy fresh produce from faraway places.

Change from the usual peas and carrots by introducing your family to vegetables that may be less familiar. Try Brussels Sprouts in Mustard Sauce, Leeks with Pepper Sauce, Beets with Raisins or Eggplant Casserole.

An easy way to increase your consumption of vegetables is to simply take your favorite casserole or stir-fry recipe and reduce the meat by half and double the vegetables.

One nice way to prepare all types of vegetables is steaming them. You don't need any special equipment although steamers are very handy. Simply place vegetables of uniform size in a vegetable-steamer basket, strainer or on a rack above a small amount of simmering water. Cover and cook until they are the desired tenderness, adding more water if needed. The water may be seasoned with a tablespoon of lemon juice or wine or by the addition of herbs. Once again be inventive—my recipes are just a guide to get you started in creative cooking. Serve steamed vegetables plain or adorned with seasonings, yogurt or dressing.

I like to serve at least two vegetables of contrasting color and texture with dinner. Think of the dinner plate as a painting: vegetables supply the accents that complete the picture; they please the eye as well as the palate.

Beets with Raisins

A bright vegetable side dish to serve with broiled meat or poultry.

1 (16-oz.) can sliced beets

1/2 cup reserved beet juice

4 teaspoons cornstarch

1/4 cup corn syrup

3 tablespoons lemon juice

1 tablespoon cider vinegar

1 teaspoon lemon peel

1/4 cup chopped onion

1/4 cup raisins

Drain juice from beets, reserving 1/2 cup. Pour reserved beet juice into a saucepan with cornstarch, stir until dissolved. Add corn syrup. lemon juice, vinegar, lemon peel and onions. Cook over medium heat until sauce thickens. Add beets and raisins. Pour mixture into a casserole, bake at 350F (175C) about 25 minutes. Makes 4 servings.

Each serving contains:

Cal	Prot	Carb	Fib	Tot. Fat	Sat. Fat	Chol	Sodium
134	2g	35g	3g	0	0	0	322mg

Brussels Sprouts in Mustard Sauce

A mild mustard sauce adds zest to the Brussels sprouts.

1 (10-oz.) pkg. frozen or 3/4 lb. fresh Brussels sprouts

1/2 cup chicken broth

1 teaspoon canola oil

2 tablespoons chopped green onion

1 cup chicken broth

1 teaspoon Dijon-style mustard

1/2 teaspoon pepper

1 tablespoon cornstarch

1/2 cup evaporated skimmed milk

Cook Brussels sprouts in 1/2 cup chicken broth; cover and set aside. Spray a small skillet with vegetable cooking spray. Add oil and sauté onion. Remove from heat and slowly add 1 cup chicken broth. Stir in mustard and pepper. Return to heat. Dissolve cornstarch in milk. Pour into mixture. Stirring constantly, cook until sauce is smooth and thickened, about 5 minutes. Pour mustard sauce over cooked Brussels sprouts and stir to coat. Serve at once. Makes 4 servings.

Each serving contains:

Cal	Prot	Carb	Fib	Tot. Fat	Sat. Fat	Chol	Sodium
94	7g	13g	4g	2g	0	2mg	75mg

Brussels Sprouts with Currants

The addition of currants makes this a special side dish.

1-1/4 cups chicken broth

1 tablespoon chopped onion

2 tablespoons dried currants

1 lb. fresh or 1 (16-oz.) pkg. frozen Brussels sprouts

2 teaspoons cornstarch

1/4 cup water

1/4 teaspoon poultry seasoning

Salt and pepper to taste

Combine chicken broth, onions, currants and Brussel sprouts in a saucepan. Cook until Brussels sprouts are tender, about 15 minutes. Remove Brussels sprouts to serving dish, cover and set aside. Dissolve cornstarch in water, add poultry seasoning and stir into cooking liquid. Stir constantly until thickened slightly. Season to taste with salt and pepper. Pour over Brussels sprouts. Serve at once. Makes 6 servings.

Each serving contains:

Cal	Prot	Carb	Fib	Tot. Fat	Sat. Fat	Chol	Sodium
52	4g	10g	4g	1g	0	0	19mg

Red Cabbage à la Orange

A pretty side dish to serve with Stuffed Pork Tenderloin, page 168.

1 tablespoon canola oil

1 onion, chopped

1 lb. red cabbage, shredded, cored

2 apples, cored, sliced

1/2 cup tomato juice

1/4 teaspoon ground cloves

1 cinnamon stick

1/2 cup red wine

1/2 cup orange marmalade

In a large skillet or Dutch oven heat oil. Sauté onion. Stir in cabbage and apples, stir fry until cabbage wilts. Add tomato juice, cloves and cinnamon stick. Cover and simmer about 10 minutes. Add wine and marmalade, mix and cook about 5 minutes longer. Serve hot or cold. Makes 6 servings.

Each serving contains:

Cal	Prot	Carb	Fib	Tot. Fat	Sat. Fat	Chol	Sodium
165	2g	34g	4g	3g	0	0	90mg

Betty's English Carrots

This is an old family recipe, handed down for generations.

2 cups (4-5) sliced carrots

1 cup small boiling onions

1 cup apple juice

1 firm apple (Granny Smith), sliced in twelfths

1 teaspoon cornstarch

1/4 cup apple juice

In a saucepan cook carrots and onions in 1 cup apple juice until tender. Add apple slices and cook until apples are tender. Dissolve cornstarch in 1/4 cup apple juice and add to mixture. Cook and stir about 5 minutes until slightly thickened. Makes 6 servings.

Each serving contains:

Cal	Prot	Carb	Fib	Tot. Fat	Sat. Fat	Chol	Sodium
77	1g	19g	3g	0	0	0	37mg

Eggplant Casserole

Subtle flavors work well together, serve with Island Slaw, page 47, or a mixed green salad.

1 lb. eggplant, cut in 8 slices

Salt

2 tablespoons canola oil

2 green onions, chopped

2 garlic cloves, minced

4 teaspoons cornstarch

1/2 cup orange juice

1/2 cup chicken broth

1/2 cup evaporated skimmed milk

1/2 teaspoon poultry seasoning

1/4 teaspoon pepper

1 teaspoon orange peel

1 cup sliced mushrooms

1 cup chopped, cooked, skinned chicken breast

2 cups cooked rice

2 tomatoes

Sprinkle eggplant with salt, set aside 30 minutes. Pat with paper towel to remove excess moisture. Brush slices with 1 tablespoon oil and place on a baking sheet. Broil 5 minutes, turn and broil other side. In a small skillet heat remaining tablespoon oil and sauté onion and garlic. Dissolve cornstarch in orange juice; stir into onion and garlic. Add milk, poultry seasoning, pepper and orange peel. When mixture has thickened, add mushrooms and chicken. Stir to combine. Spoon rice into a 13 x 9-inch baking dish. Place eggplant slices in one layer over rice. Cut each tomato in 4 thick slices. Top each eggplant slice with a tomato slice. Pour mushroom-chicken sauce over all. Cover with foil and bake 30 minutes in a 350F (175C) oven. Makes 8 servings.

Each serving contains:

Cal	Prot	Carb	Fib	Tot. Fat	Sat. Fat	Chol	Sodium
168	8g	25g	3g	4g	0	12mg	34mg

Spicy Green Beans

Cauliflower and carrots can be treated in the same manner.

2 lbs. fresh or 2 (10-oz.) pkgs. frozen green beans

1 cup chopped jícama or water chestnuts

2 tablespoons chopped fresh parsley

3 tablespoons chopped pimiento-stuffed olives

1/2 cup Italian Dressing, page 63

Trim ends of fresh green beans. Cook with water to cover 10 to 12 minutes, until tender-crisp, drain. If using frozen, cook according to package directions, drain. Combine beans, jícama or water chestnuts, parsley and olives in a shallow bowl. Pour Italian Dressing over bean mixture. Cover and refrigerate at least 2 hours. Stir twice while chilling. Makes 6 servings.

Each serving contains:

Cal	Prot	Carb	Fib	Tot. Fat	Sat. Fat	Chol	Sodium
98	3g	13g	4g	5g	1g	0	61mg

Leeks with Tarragon-Pepper Sauce

Looks like a giant green onion, but it's sweeter and milder.

8 leeks

1-1/2 cups chicken broth

1 teaspoon dried-leaf tarragon

1/4 cup vermouth or lemon juice

1/2 cup chopped red bell pepper

2 tablespoons cornstarch

1/4 cup skim milk

1 tablespoon chopped chives

Salt and pepper to taste

Trim dark green portion and roots from leeks. Cut in half lengthwise; thoroughly rinse to remove dirt. In a large skillet heat chicken broth, add leeks; cover and simmer 7 to 10 minutes or until tender. Remove leeks to a serving dish; cover and keep warm. Add tarragon and vermouth or lemon juice and bell peppers to broth. Dissolve cornstarch in milk. Stir into broth. Continue stirring until thickened. Add chives. Season to taste with salt and pepper. Pour sauce over leeks. Serve at once. Makes 4 servings.

Each serving contains:

Cal	Prot	Carb	Fib	Tot. Fat	Sat. Fat	Chol	Sodium
155	5g	29g	4g	1g	0	1mg	45mg

Mushroom Casserole

Serve with Rosemary-Orange Chicken, page 189.

1 lb. medium mushrooms, whole

1 onion, sliced

2 tomatoes, quartered

1 tablespoon lemon peel

1/2 teaspoon dried-leaf oregano

1/2 teaspoon dill weed

1/2 teaspoon garlic powder

1 tablespoon sunflower seeds

Wipe mushrooms with a damp cloth or paper towel. Trim stems. Spray a baking dish with olive-oil cooking spray. Place mushrooms, onions and tomatoes in prepared dish. Sprinkle with lemon peel, oregano, dill weed, garlic powder and sunflower seeds. Bake uncovered about 20 minutes in a 350F (175C) oven. Serve at once. Makes 4 servings.

Each serving contains:

Cal	Prot	Carb	Fib	Tot. Fat	Sat. Fat	Chol	Sodium
68	4g	12g	4g	2g	0	0	11mg

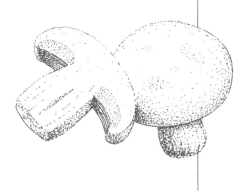

Stuffed Peppers Florentine

When available, use red and yellow bell peppers.

1 (10-oz.) pkg. frozen chopped spinach

1/2 lb. select extra-lean ground beef

1 garlic clove, minced

1 small onion, minced

1/4 teaspoon dried-leaf basil

1/4 teaspoon dried-leaf oregano

2 tablespoons raisins

1/2 cup cooked brown rice

2 tablespoons tomato paste

1 egg white, slightly beaten

4 green bell peppers, seeded, stems removed

2 teaspoons chopped pimento

2 teaspoons chopped parsley

Preheat oven to 375F (190C). Spray a 8 x 10-inch baking dish with olive-oil vegetable cooking spray. Cook spinach according to package instructions. Drain, squeezing out as much liquid as possible. Set aside. Spray a skillet with olive-oil cooking spray. Add beef, garlic and onion. Cook until beef is browned; drain excess fat. In a large bowl combine spinach, beef, basil, oregano, raisins, rice, tomato paste and egg white. Fill peppers with mixture and top with pimento and parsley. Place in prepared baking dish. Bake about 30 minutes. Makes 4 servings.

Each serving contains:

Cal	Prot	Carb	Fib	Tot. Fat	Sat. Fat	Chol	Sodium
255	19g	22g	4g	11g	4g	49mg	128mg

Potato Sticks

Serve these wedges with Hamburgers Deluxe, page 231, or California Chicken Sandwich, page 232.

2 large baking potatoes, unpeeled

2 tablespoons olive oil

1 teaspoon dried-leaf oregano

1 teaspoon paprika

Salt and pepper to taste

Preheat oven to 425F (220C). Scrub potatoes, pat dry. Cut into eighths. Brush with oil and place in a baking dish. Sprinkle with oregano and paprika. Bake about 35 minutes until potatoes are done. Season to taste with salt and pepper. Makes 4 servings.

Each serving contains:

Cal	Prot	Carb	Fib	Tot. Fat	Sat. Fat	Chol	Sodium
172	2g	26g	3g	7g	1g	0	8mg

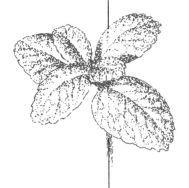

Twice-Baked Potatoes

Make ahead, cover and refrigerate until ready to heat.

3 medium baking potatoes

1/4 cup plain nonfat yogurt

1/2 cup nonfat cottage cheese

1 tablespoon chopped chives or green onions

1/4 teaspoon dill weed

1 teaspoon dried-leaf basil

2 teaspoons chopped fresh parsley

1/4 cup grated Parmesan cheese

2 tablespoons chopped pistachios

Paprika

Bake potatoes at 425F (220 C) about 1 hour. Remove from oven and slice in half lengthwise. Carefully scoop out potato pulp, leaving the shell intact. Place shells on a baking sheet.

In a large bowl mash potato pulp with yogurt, cottage cheese, chives or green onion, dill weed, basil, parsley and 2 tablespoons Parmesan cheese. Fill potato shells, mounding mixture. Sprinkle with remaining cheese, pistachios and paprika. Bake at 375F (190C) 15 to 20 minutes until heated through. Makes 6 servings.

Each serving contains:

Cal	Prot	Carb	Fib	Tot. Fat	Sat. Fat	Chol	Sodium
159	7g	28g	3g	2g	1g	4mg	149mg

Squash-Cheese Casserole

A colorful medley of vegetables, sure to please most everyone.

2 crookneck squash, sliced

2 pattypan squash, sliced

2 tomatoes, sliced

1 (12-oz.) can cream-style corn, drained

3 green onions, chopped

6 (2/3-oz.) slices lowfat American cheese

2 teaspoons chopped cilantro (Chinese parsley)

1 teaspoon dried-leaf oregano

1 teaspoon dried-leaf marjoram

Salt and pepper to taste

Preheat oven to 350F (175C). Spray a 2-quart casserole with vegetable cooking spray. Combine squash, tomatoes, corn and green onions. Cover and bake 20 minutes. Place cheese slices in one layer over vegetables. Combine cilantro, oregano and marjoram and scatter on top of cheese. Bake uncovered 10 to 12 minutes. Season to taste with salt and pepper. Makes 6 servings.

Each serving contains:

Cal	Prot	Carb	Fib	Tot. Fat	Sat. Fat	Chol	Sodium
103	2g	16g	3g	3g	0	10mg	447mg

Zucchini-Onion Casserole

If available, use both yellow and green zucchini.

2 tablespoons canola oil

2 cups zucchini slices

1 cup onion slices

1/2 cup sliced mushrooms

2 tablespoons cornstarch

2/3 cup chicken broth

1/4 cup dry sherry

1 teaspoon dill weed

1/2 teaspoon paprika

3 tablespoons bread crumbs

2 tablespoons grated Parmesan cheese

Heat oil, sauté zucchini and onion, stir in mushrooms. Spray a baking dish with vegetable cooking spray. Transfer zucchini mixture to baking dish. In a cup combine cornstarch with chicken broth, sherry, dill weed and paprika. Pour over zucchini. Combine bread crumbs and Parmesan cheese. Sprinkle on top. Bake in 350F (175C) oven about 25 minutes. Makes 4 to 6 servings.

Each serving contains:

Cal	Prot	Carb	Fib	Tot. Fat	Sat. Fat	Chol	Sodium
91	2g	6g	1g	5g	1g	1mg	42mg

Baked Vegetable Medley

Use fresh vegetables to replace frozen if you prefer.

1 (16-oz.) pkg. frozen mixed vegetables

1 cup beef broth

1/2 teaspoon dried-leaf basil

1/2 teaspoon dried-leaf tarragon

2 teaspoons chopped fresh parsley

Preheat oven to 350F (175C). Combine all ingredients in a shallow baking dish. Bake covered about 15 minutes. Serve hot or cold. Makes 5 servings.

Each serving contains:

Cal	Prot	Carb	Fib	Tot. Fat	Sat. Fat	Chol	Sodium
58	3g	12g	4g	0	0	0	32mg

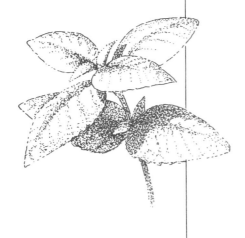

Vegetables with Dill

A colorful medley of favorite vegetables.

1/2 lb. small whole onions, peeled

1 lb. small new potatoes, cubed

6 carrots, peeled and cut into 1-inch pieces

1 cup chicken broth

1 teaspoon dill weed or 2 tablespoons fresh, chopped dill

1 cup frozen peas

Spray a Dutch oven or heavy, large saucepan with butter-flavor vegetable cooking spray. Sauté onions until lightly browned. Add all remaining ingredients except peas; heat to boiling. Reduce to simmer, cover and cook 30 to 45 minutes, until vegetables are tender. Add peas and cook 5 minutes longer. Makes 6 servings.

Each serving contains:

Cal	Prot	Carb	Fib	Tot. Fat	Sat. Fat	Chol	Sodium
136	5g	29g	5g	1g	0	0	57mg

Marinated Vegetables

Vary the beans to suit your family's choice. This can be refrigerated several days.

1 (16-oz.) can kidney beans, drained

1 (16-oz.) can lima beans, drained

1 (16-oz.) can black-eyed peas, drained

1 red bell pepper, sliced

1 onion, sliced

1/3 cup sugar

1/2 cup wine or cider vinegar

1/3 cup olive oil

1/2 teaspoon dry mustard

1/2 teaspoon dried-leaf marjoram

1/2 teaspoon dried-leaf basil

2 tablespoons chopped fresh parsley

Rinse drained beans with water and drain again. In a serving bowl combine all ingredients. Cover and marinate at least 6 hours. Serve chilled as a side dish or on lettuce leaves as a salad. Makes 6 to 8 servings.

Each serving contains:

Cal	Prot	Carb	Fib	Tot. Fat	Sat. Fat	Chol	Sodium
356	12g	51g	18g	13g	2g	0	665mg

Fish & Seafood

The bounty of the sea is waiting for you at your market. Although fresh seafood is preferred, it's not always available. Fortunately, frozen can be a very satisfactory substitute. Modern processing at sea results in very quick freezing, which helps preserve flavor and texture.

If you have a fisherman in the family, encourage him to bring the catch home. To freeze fish at home—slower than commercial freezing—place fish in a shallow pan, fill with water, cover with foil and freeze. After frozen solid, transfer to a plastic freezer bag. Try to include fish in your diet two or three times a week.

Ease of preparation and short cooking time make fish or seafood an ideal choice. Choose to bake, broil, poach, stir-fry or steam your favorite fish. For best results cook fish on high heat for a short time because overcooking both toughens and dries the fish.

And don't overlook the benefits of omega-3—a very, very good fat—gained by eating these foods. Herring, mackerel, salmon, trout and white tuna are some of the best sources of omega-3 fatty acids. However these benefits can be lost when the fish is deep fried and heavily sauced with butter or cream.

Enjoy the Crab and Pasta if you are in the mood for something cold. Or for a special dish, Orange Roughy in Parchment or Fillets Pacifica vie for the number-one choice. Tender Scallop Kabobs taste so great that no one will suspect it was prepared in minutes. If you are a salmon lover, treat yourself to the Salmon with Curry Sauce.

Baked Fish Pizzaiola

An uncomplicated dish that tastes simply great.

1 lb. flounder fillets

1 garlic clove, minced

1/2 teaspoon dried-leaf basil

Fresh ground black pepper to taste

1-1/2 cups diced fresh tomato

2 green onions, diced

2 tablespoons chopped fresh Italian parsley

Preheat oven to 425F (220C). Spray a baking dish with olive-oil vegetable cooking spray. Place fillets in single layer in baking dish. Spray fillets with olive-oil vegetable cooking spray. Sprinkle minced garlic, basil and pepper over fish. Arrange tomatoes and onions over fish. Sprinkle with parsley. Cover with foil. Bake 10 to 15 minutes or until fish flakes. Makes 4 servings.

Each serving contains:

Cal	Prot	Carb	Fib	Tot. Fat	Sat. Fat	Chol	Sodium
120	22g	4g	1g	2g	0	54mg	99mg

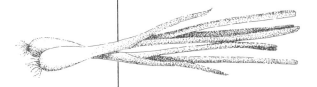

Baked Catfish Fillets

A crisp coating without frying.

1 lb. skinless catfish fillets

1/2 cup evaporated skimmed milk

1/3 cup cornmeal

1/2 teaspoon paprika

1 teaspoon dill weed

1/4 teaspoon garlic powder

Rinse fillets and pat dry. Set aside. Spray a baking dish with olive-oil vegetable cooking spray. Preheat oven to 425F (220C). Pour milk into a shallow dish or pie plate. Combine cornmeal, paprika, dill weed and garlic in another dish. Dip fillets in milk and then in cornmeal mixture. Place in prepared baking dish. Lightly spray with olive-oil cooking spray. Bake uncovered 10 to 12 minutes or until fish flakes. Makes 4 servings.

Each serving contains:

Cal	Prot	Carb	Fib	Tot. Fat	Sat. Fat	Chol	Sodium
200	24g	13g	1g	5g	1g	67mg	109mg

Clams
in Tomato Sauce

Delicious and easy to prepare in less than 30 minutes.

2 teaspoons olive oil

1 garlic clove

1/4 onion, chopped

1/4 green bell pepper, chopped

2 teaspoons chopped parsley

1/2 teaspoon dried-leaf basil

1 large tomato, chopped, seeded

1/2 teaspoon sugar, if desired

1 (6-oz). can clams

1/2 cup frozen peas

Cooked pasta

4 teaspoons grated Parmesan cheese

In a skillet heat oil, sauté garlic, onion and bell pepper. Stir in parsley, basil, tomato and sugar if desired. Reduce heat, add clams with juice. Cover and simmer 15 minutes. Add peas, cook 5 minutes. Serve over cooked pasta and sprinkle with Parmesan cheese. Makes 4 servings.

Each serving contains:

Cal	Prot	Carb	Fib	Tot. Fat	Sat. Fat	Chol	Sodium
121	13g	8g	2g	4g	1g	30mg	83mg

Caribbean Cod

Steamed rice and fresh fruit slices complete this meal.

1 lb. poached boneless cod

2 tablespoons olive oil

4 garlic cloves

1/2 onion, sliced

3 tomatoes, chopped

1/4 teaspoon chile-pepper flakes

1 tablespoon capers

2 tablespoons sliced olives

1 tablespoon blanched slivered almonds

2 tablespoons chopped parsley

Cut poached cod into bite-size pieces, set aside. In a skillet heat oil and garlic cloves. When garlic turns golden, remove from oil and discard. Add onions and sauté. Add tomatoes, chile-pepper flakes and capers. Reduce heat, cover and cook about 15 minutes. Add olives, almonds, parsley and reserved cod. Heat through. Serve at once. Makes 4 servings.

Each serving contains:

Cal	Prot	Carb	Fib	Tot. Fat	Sat. Fat	Chol	Sodium
226	27g	8g	2g	10g	1g	62mg	160mg

Cod with Ginger Grapefruit

Mild-flavored cod with a flavorful sauce.

1/4 cup grapefruit juice

1/4 cup orange juice

1 teaspoon grated ginger root

1 teaspoon grated orange peel

1 green onion, chopped

1 garlic clove, minced

1/2 teaspoon sesame oil

1 lb. cod, halibut or orange roughy fillets

1 tomato, sliced

1 grapefruit, segmented

Spray a baking dish with vegetable cooking spray. In a bowl combine grapefruit juice, orange juice, ginger root, orange peel, green onion, garlic and sesame oil. Place cod in baking dish. Pour mixture over. Turn cod to coat both sides. Cover and refrigerate about 20 minutes. Remove cover and top cod with tomato slices and grapefruit segments. Spoon sauce over tomatoes. Bake uncovered at 425F (220C) about 10 minutes. Makes 4 servings.

Each serving contains:

Cal	Prot	Carb	Fib	Tot. Fat	Sat. Fat	Chol	Sodium
138	21g	10g	1g	2g	0	49mg	65mg

Crab and Pasta

Enjoy this as a main dish for lunch or a light supper.

1/2 cup cooked pinto beans, drained

1 (6-oz.) can crab or water-pack tuna

2 green onions, chopped

1 small zucchini, thinly sliced

2 tomatoes, chopped

2 tablespoons chopped sweet pickles

2 cups cooked mostaccioli pasta

1/3 cup Italian Dressing, page 63

Rinse and drain beans. In a large bowl combine crab or tuna, beans, green onions, zucchini, tomatoes and pickles. Add hot cooked pasta. Toss all together with Italian Dressing. Serve at once, or cover and refrigerate 2 hours to thoroughly chill. Makes 6 servings.

Each serving contains:

Cal	Prot	Carb	Fib	Tot. Fat	Sat. Fat	Chol	Sodium
159	10g	21g	3g	4g	1g	25mg	138mg

Fillets Pacifica

Popular flavors borrowed from the Pacific Rim.

1 lb. white fish fillets

1/4 cup low-sodium soy sauce

2 tablespoons lemon juice

1 tablespoon canola oil

1 teaspoon grated fresh ginger root

1 teaspoon brown sugar

1 green onion, sliced

1 teaspoon toasted sesame seeds

Arrange fish in shallow dish. Combine soy sauce, lemon juice, oil, ginger root, brown sugar and green onion. Pour over fish. Cover and refrigerate at least one hour. Drain fish; reserve marinade. Broil fish about 3 inches from heat 3 to 4 minutes on each side. Brush with sauce at least one time. Sprinkle with sesame seeds. Makes 4 servings.

Each serving contains:

Cal	Prot	Carb	Fib	Tot. Fat	Sat. Fat	Chol	Sodium
154	23g	3g	0	5g	1g	54mg	1125mg

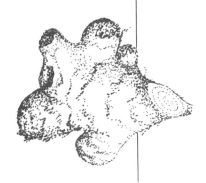

Dilled Halibut Steaks

A bit more flair and flavor than plain broiled fish.

2 tablespoons lemon juice

2 tablespoons celery leaves

1 bay leaf

1 quart water

1 lb. halibut steaks, about 1-inch thick

1/3 cup lowfat plain yogurt

3 tablespoons reduced-calorie mayonnaise

1/2 teaspoon dill weed

2 teaspoons minced chives

1/4 teaspoon salt

1/4 teaspoon pepper

1/4 teaspoon paprika

Lemon wedges

In a large skillet combine lemon juice, celery leaves, bay leaf and water. Bring to a boil. Add halibut steaks; cover and simmer 4 minutes or until barely done. With slotted spoon or spatula, carefully lift fish out of water; place in broiler pan. In a small bowl combine yogurt, mayonnaise, dill weed, chives, salt, pepper and paprika. Spread over top of each steak. Broil 5 or 6 inches from heat source until bubbly and golden on top. Garnish with lemon wedges. Makes 4 servings.

Each serving contains:

Cal	Prot	Carb	Fib	Tot. Fat	Sat. Fat	Chol	Sodium
164	25g	4g	0	5g	1g	39mg	265mg

Mahi Mahi Español

Try this delicate-flavored fish from the Pacific.

2 teaspoons olive oil

3 garlic cloves, chopped

1 onion, chopped

4 (1 lb.) tomatoes, chopped

1 green or red bell pepper, chopped, or 1 green chile pepper, chopped

3 tablespoons chopped parsley

1/2 teaspoon ground cinnamon

1 lb. mahi mahi, cut in 1-inch cubes

2 tablespoons chopped toasted almonds, sliced

In a skillet heat oil, sauté garlic and onions. Add tomatoes, peppers or green chiles and parsley. Cook together 3 to 4 minutes. Stir in cinnamon. Add fish cubes, cover and cook 10 minutes. Sprinkle with almonds. Makes 4 servings.

Each serving contains:

Cal	Prot	Carb	Fib	Tot. Fat	Sat. Fat	Chol	Sodium
191	24g	12g	3g	6g	1g	83mg	114mg

Orange Roughy in Parchment

Make packets of parchment or foil for no-mess baking.

1 carrot, julienned

6 whole Chinese pea pods

2 (6-oz.) orange roughy fillets

1/4 cup lime juice

Paprika

2 tablespoons sliced pimiento-stuffed olives

2 tablespoons capers

2 tablespoons chopped parsley

Preheat oven to 425F (220C). Cook carrots in 1/2 cup water for 5 minutes. Drain and set aside. Cut parchment or foil into pieces large enough to wrap each fillet. Place one half carrots and pea pods in center of foil. Place 1 fillet on top of carrots. Pour lime juice over fillets and sprinkle with paprika. Scatter olives on top and sprinkle with capers and parsley. Fold parchment edges together, roll and fold to seal. Place on a baking sheet and bake 8 to 10 minutes. To serve, place packet on serving dish, cut a slash on top and tear open. Makes 2 servings.

Each serving contains:

Cal	Prot	Carb	Fib	Tot. Fat	Sat. Fat	Chol	Sodium
257	26g	9g	2g	13g	0	34mg	293mg

Note: Total fat and saturated fat for orange roughy may be considerably lower due to wax ester content of total lipids.

Red Snapper with Wine Sauce

Raisins and peas add color and interest to a wine sauce.

1 teaspoon olive oil

1 green onion, chopped

1/4 cup red bell pepper, sliced

1 garlic clove, minced

2 tablespoons raisins

1/4 teaspoon ground cinnamon

3/4 cup white wine

1/2 cup frozen petite peas

1 lb. red snapper fillets

Preheat oven to 450F (230C). In a small skillet heat oil and sauté green onion, red bell pepper and garlic. Add raisins, cinnamon, wine and peas. Spray a baking dish with vegetable cooking spray. Rinse fillets and pat dry. Place in baking dish. Spoon wine mixture over fillets. Cover and bake 5 minutes; remove cover. Spoon sauce over fish and bake another 5 minutes. Serve with sauce. Makes 4 servings.

Each serving contains:

Cal	Prot	Carb	Fib	Tot. Fat	Sat. Fat	Chol	Sodium
187	25g	8g	2g	3g	1g	42mg	96mg

Broiled Red Snapper

A creamy topping with a blush of color.

1/3 cup plain lowfat yogurt

1 tablespoon tomato sauce

1/2 teaspoon paprika

1 tablespoon capers

2 teaspoons fresh chopped parsley

3/4 lb. red snapper fillets

In a cup mix yogurt, tomato sauce, paprika, capers and parsley. Spray a broiling pan with vegetable cooking spray. Place fillets on broiler pan; spread fillet tops with yogurt mixture. Broil without turning 6 to 8 minutes, until done. Makes 4 servings.

Each serving contains:

Cal	Prot	Carb	Fib	Tot. Fat	Sat. Fat	Chol	Sodium
98	19g	2g	0	1g	0	32mg	92mg

Salmon with Curry Sauce

A mild curry sauce is a natural for the delicate salmon flavor.

1 lb. salmon fillets

1 teaspoon canola oil

Curry Sauce:
1 tablespoon canola oil

1 tablespoon chopped chives

1 tablespoon curry powder

1 teaspoon dry mustard

1/4 cup white wine

2 tablespoons lemon juice

1 tablespoon dried currants

1 teaspoon cornstarch

3/4 cup evaporated skimmed milk

Spray a broiler pan with vegetable cooking spray. Rinse fillets and pat dry. Brush fillets with 1 teaspoon oil and broil about 10 minutes per inch of fish. In a small skillet heat 1 table-spoon oil. Stir in chives, curry powder and mustard. Blend thoroughly. Remove from heat; stirring constantly add wine and lemon juice. Return to heat and add currants. Dissolve cornstarch in milk; stir into curry mixture. Blend. Remove broiled fish to serving dishes and top with curry sauce. Serve at once. Makes 4 servings.

Each serving contains:

Cal	Prot	Carb	Fib	Tot. Fat	Sat. Fat	Chol	Sodium
263	26g	9g	1g	12g	1g	64mg	107mg

Scallop Kabobs

The delicate flavor of scallops is accented by the Italian Dressing.

1 cup Italian Dressing, page 63

1 lb. scallops

1 small onion, quartered

1 red bell pepper

12 small fresh mushrooms

1 green bell pepper

Cooked rice

Pour Italian Dressing into a medium bowl. Add scallops and onion, toss to coat all pieces. Cover and refrigerate at least 2 hours. Preheat broiler. Alternate scallops, onion, red pepper, mushroom and green pepper on skewers. Broil, turning often, about 7 minutes. Serve with steamed rice. Makes 4 servings.

Each serving contains:

Cal	Prot	Carb	Fib	Tot. Fat	Sat. Fat	Chol	Sodium
242	20g	8g	1g	15g	2g	37mg	198mg

Sea Bass in Salsa

Choose the level of hotness by selecting either the mild Anaheim Chile or the hotter Jalapeño.

1 cup chopped tomatoes

1 cup chopped fresh tomatillos

1/4 onion, chopped

1 mild or jalapeño chile pepper, chopped

1/2 teaspoon dried-leaf oregano

Salt and pepper to taste

1 lb. sea bass fillets

Spray a skillet with olive-oil cooking spray. Add tomatoes, tomatillos and onions. Cook and stir 3 to 5 minutes. Add chile pepper, oregano and salt and pepper to taste. Cook about 5 minutes longer. Preheat oven to 425F (220C). Spray a baking dish with olive oil cooking spray. Rinse fillets and pat dry. Place fillets in a single layer in prepared baking dish. Spoon tomato mixture on top. Cover and bake 10 to 15 minutes or until fish flakes. Serve at once. Makes 4 servings.

Each serving contains:

Cal	Prot	Carb	Fib	Tot. Fat	Sat. Fat	Chol	Sodium
157	23g	6g	2g	5g	1g	77mg	89mg

Shrimp Broil

*Scallops, sea bass or cod can be
substituted for shrimp.*

1 (12-oz.) can beer

1/4 teaspoon chile-pepper flakes

1/2 teaspoon dry mustard

1 tablespoon lime juice

2 green onions, chopped

1/4 teaspoon paprika

**1/2 to 3/4 lb. shrimp, peeled and
deveined, or cod**

In a bowl mix beer, chile flakes,
mustard, lime, green onions and
paprika. Add shrimp or cod, marinate 3 to 4 hours. Spray broiler pan
with vegetable spray to prevent
shrimp from sticking. Broil at 450F
(230C) or high broil 7 to 10 minutes
until done. Turn at least once, brush
with more marinade if necessary.
Serve at once. Makes 4 servings.

Each serving contains:

Cal	Prot	Carb	Fib	Tot. Fat	Sat. Fat	Chol	Sodium
98	12g	4g	1g	1g	0	86mg	89mg

Seafood and Chicken Casserole

Combine many ingredients in one great colorful dish.

2 teaspoons olive oil

1 onion, chopped

2 garlic cloves, minced

2 celery stalks, sliced

1/4 cup chopped green pepper

2 tomatoes, chopped

1 bay leaf

1 cup chicken broth

2 tablespoons tomato paste

1/2 teaspoon dried-leaf oregano

1/4 teaspoon paprika

1/2 cup dry white wine

1/2 cup diced raw scallops

1/2 cup cubed, cooked chicken

1/2 cup cubed, cooked firm fish

1/2 cup peas

1/4 cup sliced, pitted black olives

1 tablespoon capers

2 cups cooked rice

Salt and pepper to taste

In a large skillet heat oil and sauté onion and garlic. Add celery, green pepper, tomatoes, bay leaf, broth, tomato paste, oregano and paprika. Cover and simmer about 15 minutes. Stir in remaining ingredients. Spray a 2-quart baking dish with olive oil vegetable cooking spray. Spoon mixture into prepared dish. Cover with foil and bake at 350F (175C) for 25 minutes. Remove and discard bay leaf. Season to taste with salt and pepper. Makes 12 servings.

Each serving with white meat contains:

Cal	Prot	Carb	Fib	Tot. Fat	Sat. Fat	Chol	Sodium
100	5g	14g	1g	2g	0	7mg	51mg

Each serving with dark meat contains:

Cal	Prot	Carb	Fib	Tot. Fat	Sat. Fat	Chol	Sodium
102	5g	14g	1g	2g	0	8mg	52mg

Baked Sole with Carrots and Zucchini

Cook fish on high heat for a short time to keep it moist and flaky.

2 carrots, julienned

1 medium zucchini, julienned

1 lb. sole fillets

Salt and pepper to taste

1 garlic clove, minced

1/2 lemon, thinly sliced

1 tablespoon chopped fresh dill

Preheat oven to 425F (220C). Steam or parboil carrots and zucchini until tender crisp. Spray a baking dish with vegetable cooking spray, add fillets. Season to taste with salt and pepper. Sprinkle with garlic. Arrange lemon slices over fillets. Add vegetables and sprinkle dill over all. Cover loosely and bake in preheated oven 15 minutes or until fish flakes. Makes 4 servings.

Each serving contains:

Cal	Prot	Carb	Fib	Tot. Fat	Sat. Fat	Chol	Sodium
126	22g	5g	2g	1g	0	54mg	105mg

Sole Florentine

*Mushrooms and pimiento brighten
the creamed spinach filling.*

2 teaspoons olive oil

1/2 onion, chopped

1 garlic clove, minced

2 tablespoons all-purpose flour

1 cup nonfat milk

1/2 cup sliced mushrooms

2 tablespoons pimiento, chopped

1/4 teaspoon ground nutmeg

**1 (10-oz.) pkg. frozen spinach,
thawed, drained**

1 lb. sole fillets

Preheat oven to 425F (220C). In a
saucepan heat oil, sauté onion and
garlic. Stir in flour and milk. Cook,
stirring, until thickened. Stir in mushrooms, pimiento, nutmeg and spinach. Thoroughly combine. Spread
mixture on fillets. Roll up and secure
with wooden picks, place in a baking dish. Cover and bake about 15
minutes. Makes 4 servings.

Each serving contains:

Cal	Prot	Carb	Fib	Tot. Fat	Sat. Fat	Chol	Sodium
186	26g	11g	3g	4g	1g	55mg	180mg

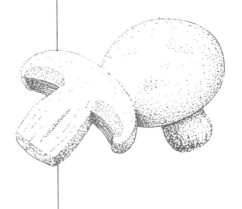

Baked White Fish

Select your favorite white fish and cereal coating.

1 lb. white fish fillets

1 tablespoon lime or lemon juice

1 egg white

1/4 teaspoon low-sodium soy sauce

1/3 cup shredded-wheat cereal crumbs

1/3 cup rice bran

1/4 teaspoon five-spice powder

Spray an 8-inch square baking dish with vegetable cooking spray. Preheat oven to 400F (205C). Rinse fish and pat dry. Drizzle lime or lemon juice over fish; set aside. In a pie plate or shallow pan lightly beat egg white and soy sauce. In another pie plate combine shredded wheat crumbs with rice bran and five-spice powder. Dip fillets in egg-white mixture, then into crumb mixture. Place in prepared dish. Bake uncovered about 15 minutes. Serve at once. Makes 4 servings.

Each serving contains:

Cal	Prot	Carb	Fib	Tot. Fat	Sat. Fat	Chol	Sodium
164	26g	7g	2g	4g	1g	36mg	97mg

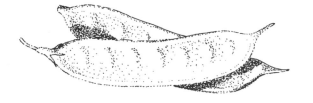

Meats

Beef is not bad—just eat less. Make it a habit to trim all visible fat from cuts of beef, pork or lamb. You can easily extend ground-meat dishes by adding 1/2 cup rice or oat bran for each pound of meat. For those who are concerned with the saturated-fat content, choose flank and top-round steaks. For easy slicing, partially freeze flank or top-round steak before attempting to cut it into thin strips. This is especially helpful when preparing stir-fry dishes. Broiled Flank Steak has a mystery ingredient that adds to the flavor.

If you have leftover steak, slice it thinly and refrigerate. Then create your own chef's salad by combining the chilled meat with vegetables and salad greens.

Lamb Kabobs are extra moist, tender and flavorful when marinated in seasoned yogurt. My Corned Leg of Lamb recipe is a variation of one from my friend Beryl Kirby in Sydney, Australia. This dish is as popular there as corned beef is in North America.

I have included pork in my choice of recipes. Because of the new methods of feeding, pork is not as fat as it was 20 years ago. The Stuffed Pork Tenderloin is a delicious entrée for entertaining. You will also find Pacific Rim Stir-Fry a great blend of Oriental flavors. Canadian bacon is also great for seasoning or as a side dish.

Three rabbit dishes are included. Rabbit is readily available, a good source of protein and similar to poultry in fat content. Rabbit dishes are appearing more often on restaurant menus, reflecting growing interest. Domestic rabbit can be found either fresh or frozen at the meat counter.

Corned Leg of Lamb

Served hot or chilled, an ideal dish for your next party.

4 lb. boneless leg of lamb

Marinade:
2 tablespoons sugar

3 garlic cloves

3 tablespoons pickle spice

1 onion, sliced

1 bay leaf

6 cloves

2 cups apple juice

Trim all visible fat from lamb. Place in a pan or dish with marinade. Cover. Marinate overnight or up to 3 days. Bring to boil, reduce heat. Cook, simmering until meat is tender, about 2 hours. Drain, discard bay leaf, serve hot or chilled. Makes 10 servings.

Each serving contains:

Cal	Prot	Carb	Fib	Tot. Fat	Sat. Fat	Chol	Sodium
299	38g	10g	0	11g	5g	122mg	95mg

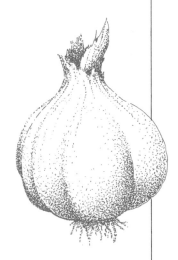

Marinated Lamb Kabobs

For a more intense flavor, refrigerate lamb in marinade for 2 days before cooking.

1/2 cup plain nonfat yogurt

1/8 teaspoon ground cinnamon

1/8 teaspoon ground cloves

2 teaspoons chopped fresh parsley

1 tablespoon lemon juice

1/2 teaspoon dried onion flakes

1/2 teaspoon fines herbs

1-1/2 lbs. boneless leg of lamb, cubed, trimmed

18 cherry tomatoes

2 green peppers, cut in cubes

1 onion, cut in 16 pieces

In a bowl combine yogurt, cinnamon, cloves, parsley, lemon juice, onion flakes and fines herbs. Add lamb and stir to coat all pieces. Cover and refrigerate 4 hours or overnight. Thread alternate pieces of lamb, tomatoes, green pepper and onion on skewers. Broil, turning several times. Makes 6 servings.

Each serving contains:

Cal	Prot	Carb	Fib	Tot. Fat	Sat. Fat	Chol	Sodium
214	28g	7g	1g	8g	3g	85mg	82mg

Lamb Patties

For those of you who like lots of spice.

3/4 lb. lean lamb, ground

4 green onions, chopped

1/4 teaspoon garlic powder

1 tablespoon fresh parsley

1/2 teaspoon paprika

1/2 teaspoon dried-leaf oregano

1/2 teaspoon chopped dried-leaf rosemary

1/4 teaspoon cumin

1 egg white

1/4 cup cooked brown rice

In a bowl thoroughly combine all ingredients. Shape into 4 patties. Broil 7 to 10 minutes on each side. Makes 4 servings.

Each serving contains:

Cal	Prot	Carb	Fib	Tot. Fat	Sat. Fat	Chol	Sodium
187	25g	4g	1g	7g	3g	76mg	75mg

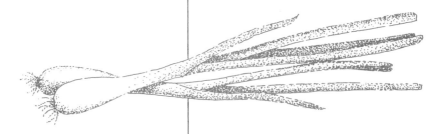

Cranberry-Wine Tenderloin

These fruit flavors enhance the tender pork.

1-1/2 lbs. trimmed, boneless pork tenderloin

2 teaspoons canola oil

1 (8-oz.) can whole cranberry sauce

1/4 cup red currant jelly

1/4 cup marsala wine

1 tablespoon lemon juice

Cut pork into 1-inch-thick slices. In a large skillet heat oil and sauté slices. In a bowl combine remaining ingredients. Remove skillet from heat and slowly add cranberry mixture. Partially cover and cook about 20 minutes, until meat is well done. Makes 6 servings.

Each serving contains:

Cal	Prot	Carb	Fib	Tot. Fat	Sat. Fat	Chol	Sodium
302	25g	25g	1g	10g	3g	62mg	66mg

Stuffed Pork Tenderloin

Ideal for that special Sunday dinner, served with steamed broccoli and Red Cabbage à la Orange, page 127.

1 teaspoon dry mustard

1/2 teaspoon dried-leaf thyme

1/2 teaspoon paprika

1/2 teaspoon garlic powder

1 teaspoon orange peel

1 lb. trimmed, boneless pork tenderloin

8 to 10 dried apricots

3 tablespoons low-sugar orange marmalade

In a cup stir together mustard, thyme, paprika, garlic powder and orange peel. Lay tenderloin open flat, sprinkle with 3/4 of herb mixture. Place apricots in a row down center of one-half of tenderloin. Lift other half over apricots and secure by tying with string at 2-inch intervals, making a firm roll. Place on a baking rack; sprinkle remaining herbs on top, patting them in. Bake at 350F (175C) about 40 minutes. Spread marmalade over top; continue baking 15 to 20 minutes. Remove from oven, cover with foil and let rest for 10 minutes before slicing. Makes 4 servings.

Each serving contains:

Cal	Prot	Carb	Fib	Tot. Fat	Sat. Fat	Chol	Sodium
255	24g	12g	1g	12g	4g	67mg	43mg

Pacific Rim Stir-Fry

Be sure to trim all the fat off pork before cutting it into strips.

3/4 cup orange juice

1/3 cup dry white wine

1 garlic clove, crushed

2 tablespoons hoisin sauce

1 tablespoon low-sodium soy sauce

1 tablespoon honey

10 oz. boneless lean pork

1 large sweet potato, peeled

2 tablespoons canola oil

1 teaspoon chicken bouillon granules

1 tablespoon cornstarch

4 green onions, cut into 1-inch lengths

1 red bell pepper, halved and sliced

1/4 lb. Chinese pea pods, trimmed

Salt and pepper to taste

3 cups cooked rice

2 nectarines, sliced

In a medium bowl combine orange juice, wine, garlic, hoisin sauce, soy sauce and honey. Cut pork into strips about 1/4 x 1/2 x 1-1/2 inches. Add to marinade, cover and refrigerate at least 1 hour. Cut sweet potato into 1/8-inch crosswise slices; halve each slice. Heat oil in a wok or large skillet. Add sweet potato slices; stir-fry 2 or 3 minutes until softened. Drain pork; reserve marinade. Add bouillon granules and cornstarch to marinade. Add drained pork to pan; cook and stir until meat is no longer pink. Stir in onions, bell pepper and reserved marinade. Cook until slightly thickened. Add pea pods. Sprinkle with salt and pepper to taste. Serve over cooked rice. Arrange sliced nectarines around each serving. Makes 4 servings.

Each serving contains:

Cal	Prot	Carb	Fib	Tot. Fat	Sat. Fat	Chol	Sodium
490	23g	67g	3g	13g	3g	39mg	884mg

Chinese Steak in Plum Sauce

Hoisin sauce is found in the Oriental food section of your supermarket.

1-1/4 lb. flank steak

Marinade:
2/3 cup plum jam

5 teaspoons hoisin sauce

1 tablespoon lemon juice

2 tablespoons cider vinegar

1/4 teaspoon powdered ginger

Trim any visible fat from steak; cut into quarters. Cut across the grain into thin diagonal strips. In a medium bowl combine all marinade ingredients. Add steak strips to marinade, tossing to coat all pieces thoroughly. Cover and refrigerate at least 30 minutes. Remove strips from marinade and thread on skewers. Broil about 2 minutes on each side. Brush with more marinade if needed. If you prefer, stir-fry rather than broil. Makes 6 servings.

Each serving contains:

Cal	Prot	Carb	Fib	Tot. Fat	Sat. Fat	Chol	Sodium
243	19g	26g	0	7g	3g	47mg	73mg

Broiled Flank Steak

Invite your guests to identify the marinade ingredients.

Marinade:
1 teaspoon instant coffee granules

2 tablespoons hot water

1 garlic clove

1/2 teaspoon dry mustard

1 teaspoon dried-leaf tarragon

2 tablespoons olive oil

2 tablespoons vermouth

2 tablespoons lemon juice

1 lb. flank steak, cut in 4 pieces

1 tablespoon cornstarch

Dissolve coffee granules in hot water. Combine remaining marinade ingredients. Place round steak in a shallow baking dish; pour marinade over steak, cover and refrigerate about 3 hours. Spray a non-stick skillet with vegetable cooking spray. Heat skillet and pan broil or place on broiler pan and cook as deserved. Dissolve cornstarch in marinade; pour in a saucepan and heat until thickened. Pour over cooked meat. Makes 4 servings.

Each serving contains:

Cal	Prot	Carb	Fib	Tot. Fat	Sat. Fat	Chol	Sodium
253	23g	3g	0	15g	5g	57mg	85mg

Stir-Fry Beef with Apricots

For best results, partially freeze steak before slicing into thin strips.

2 tablespoons canola oil

2 garlic cloves

1 tablespoon sliced fresh ginger root

1 lb. lean sirloin steak, thinly sliced

4 green onions, cut in 2-inch pieces

1/2 cup frozen peas

1/2 cup sliced water chestnuts

6 fresh apricots, pitted, sliced in half, or 1 (16-oz.) can apricots, drained

2 tablespoons chopped pistachios or walnuts

2 teaspoons cornstarch

2 tablespoons low-sodium soy sauce

2 tablespoons dry sherry

Cooked rice or noodles

Heat oil in a wok or large skillet. Cook garlic and ginger root until golden; remove and discard. Add steak slices and quickly stir-fry until meat is no longer pink, about 2 minutes. Add onions, peas and water chestnuts. Continue to stir-fry about 1 minute. Add apricots and pistachios or walnuts, stir until heated. In a cup combine cornstarch, soy sauce and sherry; stir to dissolve cornstarch. Pour into wok, stirring until slightly thickened and pieces are well coated. Serve over rice or noodles. Makes 4 servings.

Each serving contains:

Cal	Prot	Carb	Fib	Tot. Fat	Sat. Fat	Chol	Sodium
335	26g	16g	3g	18g	4g	57mg	624mg

Rabbit Provençal

Serve with noodles sprinkled with poppy seeds.

1 (2-1/2 lb.) fresh or frozen rabbit, thawed

2 tablespoons olive oil

2 tablespoons wine vinegar

1 large onion, sliced

2 bay leaves

2 garlic cloves

1 tablespoon olive oil

4 tomatoes, chopped

2/3 cup white wine

2 tablespoons parsley

Cut rabbit into serving pieces, place pieces in a bowl with 2 tablespoons olive oil, wine vinegar, onions, bay leaves and garlic. Cover and refrigerate at least 4 hours, preferably overnight, turn at least once. Remove rabbit, pat dry. Heat 1 tablespoon olive oil in a large skillet. Sauté rabbit. Add marinade mixture and remaining ingredients. Cover and simmer until tender, 40 to 45 minutes. Remove and discard bay leaves before serving. Makes 4 servings.

Each serving contains:

Cal	Prot	Carb	Fib	Tot. Fat	Sat. Fat	Chol	Sodium
506	53g	10g	2g	25g	6g	145mg	99mg

Honey Baked Rabbit

A blend of Oriental flavors adds a touch of mystery.

1 (2-1/2 lb.) fresh or frozen rabbit, thawed

1 cup wine vinegar

1 cup water

3 garlic cloves

2 bay leaves

1 onion, sliced

1/2 cup honey

3 tablespoons low-sodium soy sauce

2 tablespoons canola oil

2 tablespoons wine vinegar

3/4 teaspoon five-spice powder

Cooked wild rice

Cut rabbit into serving pieces, place pieces in a bowl with vinegar, water, garlic, bay leaves and onion. Cover and refrigerate at least 4 hours, preferably overnight. Remove and discard bay leaves. Drain rabbit, pat dry. Set aside. Spray an 10 x 8-inch baking dish with vegetable cooking spray. Set aside. Preheat oven to 350F (175C). Mix together honey, soy sauce, oil, vinegar and five-spice powder. Brush rabbit pieces with honey mixture and place in prepared baking dish. Cover and bake about 30 minutes. Turn pieces over, brushing with honey mixture; continue baking uncovered about 20 minutes. Baste with honey mixture if desired. Serve with wild rice. Makes 4 servings.

Each serving contains:

Cal	Prot	Carb	Fib	Tot. Fat	Sat. Fat	Chol	Sodium
567	53g	43g	0	21g	5g	145mg	862mg

Indian-Style Rabbit

In place of Seasoning Mix, use 2 tablespoons tandoori powder.

Seasoning Mix:

1/2 teaspoon garlic powder

1 teaspoon ground ginger

1/2 teaspoon ground coriander

1/2 teaspoon ground cumin

1/2 teaspoon turmeric

1/4 teaspoon red (cayenne) pepper

1/4 teaspoon ground cinnamon

1/4 teaspoon salt

1/2 teaspoon paprika

1/4 teaspoon ground cloves

1/2 cup nonfat yogurt

2 tablespoons lemon juice

Few drops red food coloring

1 (2-1/2 lb.) fresh or frozen rabbit, thawed

1/4 cup canola oil

1/2 cup water

Combine Seasoning Mix with yogurt, lemon juice and food coloring. Cut rabbit into serving pieces, make slashes in pieces and coat thoroughly with yogurt mixture. Cover and refrigerate at least 4 hours, preferably overnight. Heat oil in a large skillet, add rabbit pieces and brown well on both sides. Add water, cover pan, reduce heat and cook 20 minutes or until tender. Serve hot. Makes 4 servings.

Each serving contains:

Cal	Prot	Carb	Fib	Tot. Fat	Sat. Fat	Chol	Sodium
494	54g	4g	0	28g	5g	146mg	240mg

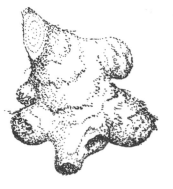

Poultry

My poultry recipes offer you the option of choosing light or dark meat. Removing the skin helps reduce the fat. For those who may not have an elevated cholesterol and prefer dark meat, I've included nutritional information for comparison. Choose whichever meets your needs. You can easily substitute chicken and turkey for other meats in many recipes.

When shopping for poultry, compare the per-pound pricing. Bear in mind that poultry skin and bones account for 60% to 70% of the total weight. Sometimes boned skinned chicken seems higher priced but may actually cost less for the edible portion.

Be guided in your purchase of poultry by the type of cooking you do. If you like to make soups and salads, the whole chicken may be your choice. Bone out the breasts and refrigerate or freeze; cook the remaining for stock. Finally, cool and bone the cooked chicken for salads or sandwiches. Always remember to skin or remove any visible fat. If you are concerned that skinned, boned poultry seems too dry, be careful not to overcook.

I think marinating helps to tenderize as well as keeps poultry moist. Marinades can be as simple as an Italian dressing, barbecue sauce or yogurt. Braising chicken is an easy and fast cooking method. Covering while cooking also helps to seal in moisture. When grilling or barbecuing, turn pieces often to assure even cooking.

Because ovens differ so much, when baking check for doneness about 10 minutes before time suggested in recipe . Boneless, skinless pieces can overcook very easily.

Personalize the recipes as you choose by using different vegetables, fruits or seasonings.

Grilled Chile Chicken

The true taste of the Southwest.

2 tablespoons lemon juice

1/2 teaspoon dried-leaf oregano

1/4 teaspoon paprika

1 lb. chicken pieces, skinned, boned

2 tablespoons canola oil

1/4 cup chopped onion

1 clove garlic, chopped

1 mild green chile, chopped

1 tomato, chopped

3 oz. mozzarella cheese, thinly sliced

1 tablespoon chopped cilantro (Chinese parsley)

Mix lemon juice, oregano and paprika. Pour over chicken; turn pieces, refrigerate 1 hour or more. Heat oil, sauté onion and garlic; add chiles and tomatoes. Broil chicken pieces, remove; place cheese on top. Spoon chile mixture on top. Return to broiler, heat until cheese melts. Sprinkle with chopped cilantro. Serve at once. Makes 4 servings.

Each serving with white meat contains:

Cal	Prot	Carb	Fib	Tot. Fat	Sat. Fat	Chol	Sodium
263	33g	5g	1g	12g	3g	77mg	189mg

Each serving with dark meat contains:

Cal	Prot	Carb	Fib	Tot. Fat	Sat. Fat	Chol	Sodium
274	29g	5g	1g	15g	4g	105mg	213mg

Chicken Cilantro

Complete this meal with Spicy Green Beans, page 130, and warm flour tortillas.

1 lb. chicken pieces, skinned, boned

1/2 teaspoon paprika

2 teaspoons canola oil

2 green onions, chopped

1/4 cup chopped cilantro (Chinese parsley) or parsley

1 tomato, chopped

1/2 cup orange juice

Sprinkle chicken pieces with paprika, patting it in. Heat oil in a skillet and brown chicken. Add remaining ingredients. Cover, reduce heat, cook about 15 minutes. Turn chicken at least twice during cooking. Makes 4 servings.

Each serving with white meat contains:

Cal	Prot	Carb	Fib	Tot. Fat	Sat. Fat	Chol	Sodium
166	27g	5g	1g	4g	1g	65mg	77mg

Each serving with dark meat contains:

Cal	Prot	Carb	Fib	Tot. Fat	Sat. Fat	Chol	Sodium
177	23g	5g	1g	7g	1g	94mg	101mg

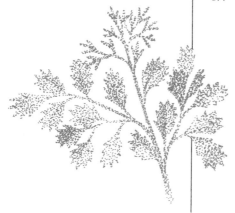

Chicken with Green Grapes

Yet another way to combine chicken and fruit.

Marinade:
2 tablespoons lemon juice

2 tablespoons cider vinegar

1 tablespoon catsup

2 teaspoons canola oil

1/4 cup white grape juice concentrate

1/4 teaspoon sweet paprika

1/2 teaspoon dry mustard

1 teaspoon dried-leaf basil

1/4 teaspoon onion powder

2 teaspoons canola oil

1 lb. boneless, skinless chicken pieces

1 cup fresh green seedless grapes

Combine marinade ingredients in a bowl. Add chicken, cover and refrigerate at least 2 hours. Spray a non-stick skillet with vegetable cooking spray. Heat; add oil and chicken pieces, lightly brown. Add marinade, cover and simmer about 15 minutes. Add grapes, cook until heated. Serve at once. Makes 4 servings.

Each serving with white meat contains:

Cal	Prot	Carb	Fib	Tot. Fat	Sat. Fat	Chol	Sodium
233	27g	18g	1g	6g	1g	65mg	121mg

Each serving with dark meat contains:

Cal	Prot	Carb	Fib	Tot. Fat	Sat. Fat	Chol	Sodium
244	23g	18g	1g	9g	2g	94mg	145mg

Apricot Pudding

A wonderful dish to make with leftover bread.

1 (14-oz.) can sweetened condensed milk

1 (14-oz.) can orange juice

2 egg whites, beaten

1/2 teaspoon almond extract

1 tablespoon grated orange peel

3 cups cubed bread

1 (16-oz.) can apricots, chopped, drained

1/3 cup toasted almonds, chopped

Apricot Sauce, page 220

Preheat oven to 350F (175C). Spray a 2-quart baking dish with butter flavored vegetable cooking spray. Pour condensed milk into a large bowl. Pour orange juice into milk can; pour juice into condensed milk, stir to blend. Fold in egg whites, almond extract and orange peel. Add bread, apricots and almonds, fold to coat all ingredients. Let stand 5 minutes; pour into prepared dish. Place a shallow pan of water on lower oven rack. Place baking dish on rack above. Bake uncovered 35 to 40 minutes. Top will be lightly browned. Remove and cool 10 minutes. Serve topped with Apricot Sauce. Makes 9 servings.

Each serving contains:

Cal	Prot	Carb	Fib	Tot. Fat	Sat. Fat	Chol	Sodium
284	8g	48g	2g	7g	3g	15mg	207mg

Baked Apple Delight

A warm breakfast or dessert to serve on a cold day.

Prune-Currant Sauce:

1 tablespoon cornstarch

1 cup apple juice

1 cup pitted prunes

1/4 cup dried currants

3 tablespoons brown sugar

1/4 teaspoon ground cloves

1 teaspoon lemon peel

2 tablespoons lemon juice

1/4 cup pecans, chopped

4 large baking apples

For Prune-Currant Sauce:
In a saucepan blend cornstarch with apple juice. Add remaining ingredients and cook, stirring constantly until sauce thickens.

For Baked Apple Delight:
Core apples and peel tops about 1 inch. Place in a shallow baking dish. Fill each cavity with Prune-Currant Sauce, reserve any remaining sauce. Bake at 350F (175C) about 60 minutes, until apples are tender. Heat remaining sauce and spoon additional sauce over baked apples. Serve warm. Makes 4 servings.

Each serving contains:

Cal	Prot	Carb	Fib	Tot. Fat	Sat. Fat	Chol	Sodium
377	3g	86g	11g	6g	1g	0	11mg

Fruit Salad Dessert

What could be simpler? Slice your fresh fruit and top it with a delicious touch of honey.

4 fresh figs, quartered

2 oranges, peeled, sliced

24 red cherries

24 green grapes

1 Granny Smith apple, sliced

Honey-Pecan Sauce:
1/4 cup honey

3/4 cup plain nonfat yogurt

2 tablespoons orange juice

1 teaspoon orange peel, grated

2 tablespoons pecans, toasted

Arrange fruit in an attractive pattern on each plate. In a small bowl combine honey, yogurt, orange juice and orange peel. Drizzle Honey-Pecan Sauce over fruit, sprinkle with pecans. Makes 4 servings.

Each serving contains:

Cal	Prot	Carb	Fib	Tot. Fat	Sat. Fat	Chol	Sodium
254	5g	57g	6g	4g	0	1mg	35mg

Minted Pears with Chocolate Sauce

Glamorize this easy-to-make, reduced-calorie, classic dessert with a sprinkling of chopped walnuts.

4 fresh pears

2 cups water

3/4 cup sugar

2 tablespoons coarsely chopped fresh mint leaves

6 drops green food coloring

2 tablespoons unsweetened cocoa powder

1/4 cup water

1/4 cup sugar

1/4 cup light corn syrup

1 tablespoon margarine

4 scoops lowfat frozen vanilla yogurt

4 teaspoons finely chopped walnuts

Peel, halve and core pears. In a 10-inch skillet combine 2 cups water, 3/4 cup sugar, mint leaves and green food coloring. Bring to a boil. Drop in pears and simmer 5 minutes; turn over in syrup and simmer another 2 or 3 minutes, or until tender. Remove from heat; refrigerate in syrup. Combine cocoa powder, 1/4 cup water, 1/4 cup sugar and corn syrup in small saucepan. Stir constantly over low heat until well blended. Simmer 2 minutes, stirring occasionally. Add margarine; set aside to cool. Drain chilled pears; discard mint leaves and liquid. Place a scoop of frozen yogurt in center of each of 4 pear halves. Top with remaining pear halves, forming 4 whole stuffed pears. Spoon about 1 tablespoon chocolate sauce into each of 4 dessert dishes. Stand 1 whole stuffed pear on end in chocolate sauce in each dessert dish. Spoon remaining chocolate sauce over each. Sprinkle with nuts. Makes 4 servings.

Each serving contains:

Cal	Prot	Carb	Fib	Tot. Fat	Sat. Fat	Chol	Sodium
465	5g	106g	6g	5g	1g	15mg	92mg

Stuffed Plums

Contrasting textures, flavors and colors create a great dessert or snack.

1/4 cup Yogurt Cream Cheese, page 3

1 tablespoon lime or orange marmalade

2 teaspoons chopped crystallized ginger

4 plums

4 teaspoons chopped pistachio nuts

✿ **Variation**
Substitute fresh apricots or peaches for plums.

In a small bowl thoroughly combine cream cheese, marmalade and ginger. Slice plums in half, set aside. Fill each plum half with cream-cheese mixture and sprinkle with nuts. Makes 4 servings.

Each serving contains:

Cal	Prot	Carb	Fib	Tot. Fat	Sat. Fat	Chol	Sodium
72	2g	14g	2g	2g	0	0	7mg

Baked Puffs

Fill these golden puffs with salad, fruit or frozen yogurt.

1/2 cup water

1/4 cup canola oil

1/2 cup all-purpose flour

1/4 teaspoon salt

1/2 cup egg substitute

Fruited Cheese Filling, page 219

Powdered sugar

Spray a cookie sheet with butter-flavor cooking spray. Set aside. Preheat oven to 425F (220C). In a medium saucepan heat water and oil to boiling. Add flour and salt all at once. Stir vigorously until flour combines making a ball. Remove from heat; let stand 5 minutes. Beat in one-half egg substitute. When thoroughly combined, beat in remaining amount. Drop by tablespoonfuls or pipe into 1-1/2-inch mounds on prepared sheet. Bake about 25 minutes until puffs are browned and appear dry. Remove and cool. Slice tops off, remove any excess inside shells. Fill with Fruited Cheese Filling. Replace top, sprinkle with powdered sugar. Makes 10 (3-inch) puffs.

Each puff contains:

Cal	Prot	Carb	Fib	Tot. Fat	Sat. Fat	Chol	Sodium
82	2g	5g	0	6g	0	0	78mg

Fruited Cheese Filling

Use as a filling for Baked Puffs, page 218, or crepes. Great on pancakes.

1 cup cream-style, lowfat cottage cheese

2 tablespoons sugar

4 teaspoons orange liqueur or juice

1/2 teaspoon vanilla extract

2/3 cup blueberries, blackberries or strawberries

3 tablespoons chopped pistachios

In a food processor, blender or mixer, combine cottage cheese, sugar, orange liqueur or juice and vanilla. Process until smooth. Rinse berries and place on paper towels, pat dry. Spoon mixture into a bowl and fold in nuts and berries. Makes about 2 cups.

Each tablespoon contains:

Cal	Prot	Carb	Fib	Tot. Fat	Sat. Fat	Chol	Sodium
15	1g	2g	0	0	0	0	29mg

Apricot Sauce

A delicious topping for Apricot Pudding, page 213.

4 oz. dried apricots

3/4 cup apple juice

1/2 cup orange juice

1/4 cup honey

2 tablespoons water

2 teaspoons cornstarch

Ground ginger to taste

Ground cinnamon to taste

1 tablespoon sweet vermouth

Cover apricots with apple juice. Bring to a full boil, then reduce heat and simmer, cover, 30 minutes. Stir apricots occasionally so they will not stick or burn. Let apricots cool, then strain. Reserve cooking liquid. Chop cooked apricots and set aside. In a 2-quart saucepan combine orange juice, honey, water, cornstarch, ginger and cinnamon. Heat, stirring constantly, until thickened slightly. Remove pan from heat and add apricots, their cooking liquid and vermouth. Serve hot or well chilled. Makes 1-1/2 cups.

Each tablespoon contains:

Cal	Prot	Carb	Fib	Tot. Fat	Sat. Fat	Chol	Sodium
30	0	8g	0	0	0	0	1mg

Cherry Sauce

*Brighten angel-food cake or frozen
yogurt with a special flavor.*

1/3 cup sugar

1-1/2 tablespoons cornstarch

1/4 teaspoon ground allspice

**1 (16-oz.) can tart pie cherries,
pitted**

1/4 cup sliced almonds

1/2 teaspoon almond extract

2 to 3 drops red food coloring

In a saucepan combine sugar, cornstarch and allspice. Drain liquid
from cherries. Set aside. Slowly stir
cherry liquid into sugar mixture.
Cook over medium heat, stirring
constantly, 5 to 7 minutes until
slightly thickened. Add cherries and
almonds; cook 2 to 3 more minutes.
Remove from heat and add almond
extract and food coloring. Makes
about 1-1/2 cups.

Each tablespoon contains:

Cal	Prot	Carb	Fib	Tot. Fat	Sat. Fat	Chol	Sodium
25	0	5g	0	1g	0	0	2mg

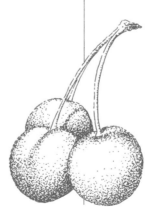

Peppermint-Stick Chocolate Mold

Angel food loaves vary in length and weight. If you have extra cake, freeze it for another time.

6 (3/4-inch-thick) crosswise slices of angel food cake

1 envelope unflavored gelatin

2 tablespoons cold water

3/4 cup sugar

3 tablespoons unsweetened cocoa powder

1/2 cup nonfat milk

1/4 cup crushed peppermint sticks or Starlight mints

1 cup plain nonfat yogurt, stirred

2 egg whites

1/8 teaspoon cream of tartar

Cut each cake slice into 3 strips about 1-1/4 x 2-3/4 x 3/4 inches. Line bottom of 8-inch springform pan with 1/2 the cake strips forming a spoke pattern. Set aside remaining strips. Sprinkle gelatin over water; let stand at least 1 minute. In a medium saucepan combine sugar and cocoa, add milk. Stir over moderate heat until smooth. Mix in dissolved gelatin. Set aside to cool about 10 minutes. Reserve 1 tablespoon crushed peppermint; add remaining candy to cocoa mixture. Stir into yogurt. Refrigerate until partially set. Beat egg whites until foamy; add cream of tartar. Beat until stiff but not dry. Fold into chocolate mixture. Spoon over cake in pan. Top with reserved cake strips in a spoke pattern. Lightly press strips until they are partially covered with chocolate mixture. Refrigerate until firm. Carefully remove sides of pan; sprinkle top with reserved peppermint. Makes one (8-inch) mold.

Each serving contains:

Cal	Prot	Carb	Fib	Tot. Fat	Sat. Fat	Chol	Sodium
227	7g	51g	1g	1g	0	1mg	248mg

Peaches & Cream Frozen Yogurt

This will become a summertime favorite with a new twist.

1 lb. fresh or 1 (1-lb.) pkg. frozen peaches, thawed

1 tablespoon cream sherry

1/2 cup honey

1 cup nonfat yogurt

1 cup evaporated skimmed milk

8 strawberries for garnish

Mint leaf for garnish

In a blender or food processor, purée peaches with cream sherry and honey. Stir in yogurt and evaporated milk. Freeze in ice-cream maker according to manufacturer's directions. Serve cold with garnish of strawberries or mint leaf. Makes 8 servings.

Each serving contains:

Cal	Prot	Carb	Fib	Tot. Fat	Sat. Fat	Chol	Sodium
132	4g	30g	1g	0	0	2mg	60mg

Strawberry Banana Frozen Yogurt

Treat yourself: use any fresh or frozen fruit that you like.

1 cup nonfat plain yogurt

1 cup nonfat milk

1/4 cup light corn syrup

1/4 cup egg substitute

1 banana

1 (10-oz.) pkg. frozen strawberries

✿ **Variation**

Lemon Supreme:
Omit corn syrup, banana and fruit; increase egg substitute to 1 cup, add 3/4 cup sugar, 1 tablespoon lemon peel, 1/3 cup lemon juice and 1 (12-oz.) can frozen juice concentrate.

Peach Melba:
Omit egg substitute and banana. Substitute 1-1/2 cups puréed peaches and use frozen raspberries.

Combine all ingredients in blender or food processor. Pour into a freezer container. For individual servings, pour into 8 (4-oz.) paper cups. Cover and freeze until firm. For a smoother texture, break into pieces and place in a mixer bowl, blender or food processor. Blend until fluffy. Makes 1 quart.

Each serving contains:

Cal	Prot	Carb	Fib	Tot. Fat	Sat. Fat	Chol	Sodium
87	4g	18g	1g	0	0	1mg	59mg

Snacks, Sandwiches & Beverages

Even though you may eat three well-rounded meals a day, there comes a time when you have a craving for that something extra. Guilt will not overtake you if that urge is satisfied with one of the following:

A cool refreshing drink as simple as a glass of club soda with fruit juice or a squeeze of lemon or lime. Or try a mixture of half soda and half chocolate milk. I have several cold drinks to choose from, including Cocoana Shake and Joyce's Pineapple Cooler.

Be prepared for sudden nibbling urges by keeping vegetable slices or sticks in the refrigerator. Reliables such as carrots and celery can be joined with zucchini, jícama or bell peppers. Enjoy them alone or with a yogurt-base dip.

Stock a variety of crackers. Crispbreads too, are available in wheat, rye and other grain combinations. Puffed rice, wheat and corn cakes can be a great base for a light, satisfying snack. Plain bagels or English muffins serve the same purpose.

Top them with sweet or savory items such as preserves, honey, fruit or chutney. If you want something less sweet, combine Yogurt Cream Cheese with garlic powder or herbs and capers. Try one of the new lowfat cheeses with salsa or mustard.

Rather than a coffee break, treat yourself to a fresh whole fruit eaten out of hand. Start with a crisp apple, a bunch of grapes or an orange cut into wedges. Although fruit juice is enjoyable, eating the whole fruit supplies extra fiber.

Air-popped popcorn can be enjoyed plain, sprinkled with Parmesan cheese and paprika or combined with dry-roasted peanuts or sunflower seeds.

Although dried fruits are not low-calorie, they are high in nutrition. I offer Fruit Bon Bons and a Trail Mix combination that's good as a snack or a topping on cold or hot cereals.

Banana-Toasted English Muffin

A special treatment for your morning muffins.

2 English muffins, sliced in half

4 teaspoons peanut butter

1 banana, thinly sliced

1 teaspoon honey

1/8 teaspoon ground cinnamon

Preheat broiler. Toast English muffin halves. Remove muffins from broiler. Spread each half lightly with peanut butter; top with banana slices. Drizzle with honey and sprinkle with cinnamon. Spray tops of muffins lightly with butter-flavor vegetable cooking spray. Return muffins to broiler until tops are browned. Makes 2 servings.

Each serving contains:

Cal	Prot	Carb	Fib	Tot. Fat	Sat. Fat	Chol	Sodium
267	8g	45g	3g	7g	1g	0	430mg

Cheese and Blueberry Muffins

Ready in minutes.

1/2 cup Yogurt Cream Cheese, page 3

1 tablespoon brown sugar

2 English muffins, split

1/2 teaspoon ground cinnamon

2 teaspoons blueberry jam

1 tablespoon chopped pecans

In a small bowl stir cream cheese, brown sugar, cinnamon and nuts. Spread mixture evenly on muffin halves. Top with jam and sprinkle with nuts. Place on a baking sheet and broil briefly until bubbly and lightly brown. Makes 2 servings.

Each serving contains:

Cal	Prot	Carb	Fib	Tot. Fat	Sat. Fat	Chol	Sodium
226	6g	41g	2g	4g	1g	1mg	404mg

Savory Cakes

Good as a snack or combine with a salad for a light lunch.

1/4 cup Yogurt Cream Cheese, page 3

1 green onion, chopped

1/4 teaspoon garlic powder

2 tablespoons mild green chile peppers

4 corn or rice cakes

1 tomato, cut in 4 slices

1/2 teaspoon dried-leaf basil

In a small bowl combine cream cheese, green onion, garlic and green chiles. Place corn or rice cakes on a baking sheet. Spread with yogurt mixture. Top with tomato slices and sprinkle with basil. Broil about 3 to 4 minutes. Serve at once. Makes 4 cakes.

Each cake contains:

Cal	Prot	Carb	Fib	Tot. Fat	Sat. Fat	Chol	Sodium
49	2g	9g	1g	0	0	0	59mg

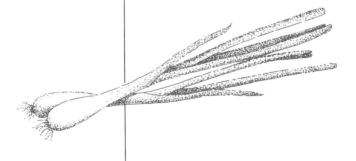

Trail Mix

You don't need to take a hike to enjoy this snack.

1/2 cup raisins

1/4 cup sunflower seeds

1/4 cup chopped walnuts

1/2 cup chopped dried apricots

1/4 cup chopped dates

1/2 cup chopped dried apples

1/4 cup peanuts

1 cup air-popped popcorn

Mix all ingredients and store in a covered container. Makes 3-1/2 cups.

Each tablespoon contains:

Cal	Prot	Carb	Fib	Tot. Fat	Sat. Fat	Chol	Sodium
19	0	3g	0	1g	0	0	1mg

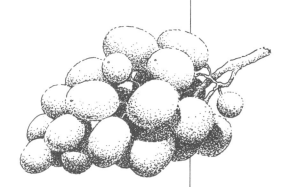

Fruit Bon Bons

Let the children help you make these no-bake treats.

2 teaspoons apple juice

1 tablespoon peanut butter

1 tablespoon honey

1/3 cup raisins

1/3 cup dates

1 tablespoon sunflower seeds

1/3 cup prunes

1/3 cup walnuts

1 tablespoon powdered sugar

1 teaspoon unsweetened cocoa powder

In a medium bowl stir together apple juice, peanut butter and honey. Combine raisins, dates, sunflower seeds, prunes and walnuts in a food processor fitted with a metal blade or in a food mill. Process or grind briefly to chop mixture. Stir into blended apple-juice mixture until well combined. Shape into 1-inch balls. In a small bowl stir powdered sugar and cocoa together. Roll fruit balls in sugar-cocoa mixture to coat. Makes 12 bon bons.

Each bon bon contains:

Cal	Prot	Carb	Fib	Tot. Fat	Sat. Fat	Chol	Sodium
80	2g	13g	2g	3g	0	0	7mg

Chile Beef and Bean Burgers

Beans provide the extra fiber, chiles the extra flavor.

6 tablespoons cooked pinto beans, drained, mashed

3/4 lb. select extra-lean beef

2 green onions, chopped

1/4 cup chopped green chiles

1-1/2 tablespoons catsup

1 teaspoon dried-leaf oregano

Salt and pepper to taste

4 English muffins, split

Lettuce

In a bowl combine all ingredients. Shape into 4 patties. Heat broiler. Spray broiler pan with vegetable cooking spray. Place patties on prepared broiler pan. Broil to desired doneness. Toast muffins, top with burger and lettuce. Makes 4 burgers.

Each burger contains:

Cal	Prot	Carb	Fib	Tot. Fat	Sat. Fat	Chol	Sodium
404	27g	33g	4g	17g	7g	74mg	513mg

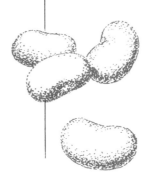

Hamburgers Deluxe

Juicy patties with wonderful flavor.

2 green onions, chopped

1 teaspoon Dijon-style mustard

1 tablespoon pickle relish

2 tablespoons tomato catsup

1/4 teaspoon garlic powder

3/4 lb. flank steak, ground

1/4 cup oat bran

4 hamburger buns

Lettuce

Alfalfa sprouts, if desired

Salt and pepper to taste

In a medium bowl combine onions, mustard, relish, catsup, garlic powder, beef and oat bran. Thoroughly mix together. Shape into 4 patties. Broil 7 to 10 minutes on each side. Slice hamburger buns in half, lightly toast. Top with meat patty, lettuce and alfalfa sprouts, if desired. Season to taste with salt and pepper. Makes 4 burgers.

Each burger contains:

Cal	Prot	Carb	Fib	Tot. Fat	Sat. Fat	Chol	Sodium
284	22g	30g	3g	9g	3g	43mg	468mg

California Chicken Sandwich

A combination of flavors that says, "California!"

2 slices sourdough bread

2 teaspoons Dijon-style mustard

1 tablespoon Green Chile Mayonnaise, page 65

3 oz. sliced, cooked chicken

1 lettuce leaf

1/2 tomato, sliced

1/4 avocado, thinly sliced

1/4 cup fresh alfalfa or bean sprouts

Lightly toast bread. Spread one slice of toasted bread with mustard. Spread another slice with Green Chile Mayonnaise. Top with lettuce, sliced chicken, tomato, avocado and alfalfa sprouts. Top with mustard-coated bread. Makes 1 sandwich.

Each sandwich with white meat contains:

Cal	Prot	Carb	Fib	Tot. Fat	Sat. Fat	Chol	Sodium
433	33g	42g	8g	15g	3g	67mg	574mg

Each sandwich with dark meat contains:

Cal	Prot	Carb	Fib	Tot. Fat	Sat. Fat	Chol	Sodium
470	30g	42g	8g	21g	5g	78g	585mg

Rosy Broiled Chicken Sandwich

The glossy marmalade topping creates a tempting look and flavor. Serve with fresh fruit slices.

4 teaspoons Dijon-style mustard

4 slices sourdough bread

4 spinach leaves

3/4 lb. sliced broiled chicken

4 tablespoons Tomato Marmalade, page 76

Spread mustard on one side of each slice of bread. Place fresh spinach leaves on top. Thinly slice broiled chicken. Spoon Tomato Marmalade on top. Makes 4 open-face sandwiches.

Each sandwich with white meat contains:

Cal	Prot	Carb	Fib	Tot. Fat	Sat. Fat	Chol	Sodium
297	28g	38g	1g	3g	1g	65mg	324mg

Each sandwich with dark meat contains:

Cal	Prot	Carb	Fib	Tot. Fat	Sat. Fat	Chol	Sodium
334	25g	38g	1g	9g	2g	76mg	335mg

Open-Face Roast Pork Sandwich

Accompany this hardy sandwich with Sunshine Salad, page 49.

4 teaspoons Dijon-style mustard

4 slices pumpernickel bread

4 lettuce leaves

4 thinly sliced Stuffed Pork Tenderloin, page 168

12 sliced pickled beets

1 onion slice, separated into rings

Dill weed

Spread mustard on one side of bread slices. Place two slices on each plate. Add a layer of lettuce and pork. Alternate beets and onions on top of pork. Sprinkle with dill weed. Makes 2 servings.

Each serving contains:

Cal	Prot	Carb	Fib	Tot. Fat	Sat. Fat	Chol	Sodium
150	10g	21g	2g	4g	1g	16mg	293mg

Tuna Fish Sandwich

Enriched with rice bran, serve open-faced or on your favorite multi-grain bread.

1 (6-oz.) can water-packed tuna, drained

1/2 teaspoon Dijon-style mustard

1 tablespoon plain nonfat yogurt

1 tablespoon reduced-calorie mayonnaise

1/4 cup rice bran

1 celery stalk, chopped

2 green onions, chopped

1 pickle, minced

1 tomato, chopped

Lettuce

8 slices whole-wheat bread

1 cup alfalfa sprouts

In a small bowl combine tuna, mustard, yogurt and mayonnaise with rice bran, celery, green onions, pickle and tomato. Place lettuce on 4 bread slices. Top with tuna and alfalfa sprouts and remaining bread slices. Makes 4 sandwiches.

Each sandwich contains:

Cal	Prot	Carb	Fib	Tot. Fat	Sat. Fat	Chol	Sodium
279	22g	41g	8g	5g	1g	25mg	722mg

Deviled Turkey Sandwiches

This filling can serve as a salad as well as a sandwich.

1 cup chopped cooked turkey

1/4 cup chopped celery

1 green onion, chopped

2 tablespoons chopped pickles

1 tablespoon chopped pimiento

1/2 teaspoon prepared horseradish

1/2 teaspoon Dijon-style mustard

2 tablespoons reduced-calorie mayonnaise

4 pita bread pockets

12 cherry tomatoes, halved

1 cucumber, sliced

4 lettuce leaves, shredded

In a small bowl mix together turkey, celery, green onion, pickles, pimiento, horseradish, mustard and mayonnaise. Cut pita breads in half, open pocket and fill with turkey mixture, tomatoes, cucumber and lettuce. Makes 4 sandwiches.

Each sandwich with white meat contains:

Cal	Prot	Carb	Fib	Tot. Fat	Sat. Fat	Chol	Sodium
275	18g	43g	3g	4g	1g	26mg	476mg

Each sandwich with dark meat contains:

Cal	Prot	Carb	Fib	Tot. Fat	Sat. Fat	Chol	Sodium
286	18g	43g	3g	5g	1g	32mg	482mg

Barbecued Turkey Burgers

For added flavor brush burgers with barbecue sauce while broiling.

3/4 lb. ground turkey

1/4 cup rice bran

2 tablespoons bottled barbecue sauce

1 teaspoon Dijon-style mustard

1 green onion, chopped

4 hamburger buns

4 teaspoons reduced-calorie mayonnaise

4 slices lowfat Cheddar cheese

Lettuce

In a bowl combine turkey, rice bran, barbecue sauce, mustard and green onion. Shape into 4 burgers. Broil as desired. Lightly spread mayonnaise on buns. Top with burger, cheese and lettuce. Makes 4 burgers.

Each burger contains:

Cal	Prot	Carb	Fib	Tot. Fat	Sat. Fat	Chol	Sodium
451	34g	28g	3g	21g	7g	80mg	649mg

Vegetarian Pita Pick-ups

They're at their very best when eaten as soon as they are prepared.

1 small cucumber

1 small red bell pepper, thinly sliced

1 carrot, peeled and shredded

1/2 cup plain nonfat yogurt

Salt and pepper to taste

3 pita bread pockets

6 lettuce leaves

2 tablespoons crumbled bleu cheese

1/4 cup chopped red onion

Cut cucumber in half lengthwise and slice thinly crosswise. In a small bowl combine cucumber, bell pepper, carrot and yogurt. Season to taste with salt and pepper. Cut each pita bread in half crosswise, insert a lettuce leaf into each half. Spoon 1/3 cup vegetable-yogurt mixture into each pita half. Top with bleu cheese and red onion. Makes 6 halves.

Each half contains:

Cal	Prot	Carb	Fib	Tot. Fat	Sat. Fat	Chol	Sodium
129	6g	22g	2g	2g	1g	4mg	257mg

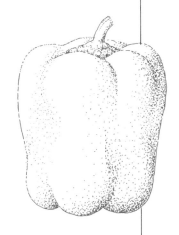

Cherry-Berry Drink

Picture pretty and tastes great.

2 to 3 ice cubes

1/2 cup cranraspberry juice

1 cup nonfat milk

1/2 cup lowfat cherry yogurt

Combine all ingredients in a blender or food processor. Blend until thoroughly combined and frothy. Serve at once. Makes 2 (8-oz.) glasses.

Each glass contains:

Cal	Prot	Carb	Fib	Tot. Fat	Sat. Fat	Chol	Sodium
143	7g	28g	0	1g	1g	5mg	96mg

Strawberry Swirl

For a special treat, substitute peaches and passion-fruit juice.

1/2 cup fresh or unsweetened strawberries

1/2 cup strawberry juice

1/4 cup evaporated skimmed milk

1/2 cup plain nonfat yogurt

2 tablespoons light corn syrup

Combine all ingredients in a blender or food processor. Blend until thoroughly combined and frothy. Serve at once. Makes 2 (10-oz.) glasses.

Each glass contains:

Cal	Prot	Carb	Fib	Tot. Fat	Sat. Fat	Chol	Sodium
150	6g	32g	1g	0	0	2mg	90mg

Cocoana Shake

Delectable as a snack or serve as a breakfast drink.

2 to 3 ice cubes

1 teaspoon unsweetened cocoa powder

3/4 cup skim milk

1/4 cup lowfat buttermilk

1 banana, peeled, sliced

2 teaspoons smooth-style peanut butter

1/4 teaspoon chocolate flavoring

Combine all ingredients in a blender or food processor. Blend until thoroughly combined, thickened and frothy. Serve at once. Makes 1 (8-oz.) glass.

Each glass contains:

Cal	Prot	Carb	Fib	Tot. Fat	Sat. Fat	Chol	Sodium
262	12g	42g	4g	7g	2g	5mg	212mg

Joyce's Pineapple Cooler

Naturally sweetened by the combination of fruits.

1/2 cup pineapple chunks

1/4 cup pineapple juice

1 small banana

2 tablespoons nonfat yogurt

3 ice cubes

Combine all ingredients in a blender or food processor. Blend until thoroughly combined and frothy. Serve at once. Makes 1 (10-oz.) glass.

Each glass contains:

Cal	Prot	Carb	Fib	Tot. Fat	Sat. Fat	Chol	Sodium
196	3g	49g	4g	1g	0	1mg	24mg

Index